Emre strand

Editor
Brent L. Fox, M. Ed.

Editor in Chief
Karen J. Goldfluss, M.S. Ed.

Creative Director
Sarah M. Fournier

Cover Artist
Diem Pascarella

Art Coordinator
Renée Mc Elwee

Illustrator
Clint McKnight

Imaging
Amanda R. Harter

Publisher
Mary D. Smith, M.S. Ed.

W0010678

GRADE 5

TCR 3834

INSTANT READING COMPREHENSION PRACTICE

- Provides 240 fiction and nonfiction quick-read activities for applying eight comprehension strategies

- Reinforces reading skills throughout the year

- Includes a "Strategies in Writing" section to practice comprehension skills in an open-ended, short-answer format

- **Correlated to Common Core State Standards**

This is a tapsponder enabled resource!

Teacher Created Resources

Authors
Ruth Foster, M. Ed.
Mary S. Jones, M. Ed.

CORRELATED TO COMMON CORE STANDARDS

For correlations to the Common Core State Standards, see pages 141–142. Correlations can also be found at *http://www.teachercreated.com/standards.*

Teacher Created Resources
6421 Industry Way
Westminster, CA 92683
www.teachercreated.com
ISBN: 978-1-4206-3834-9
© 2015 Teacher Created Resources
Made in U.S.A.

Teacher Created Resources

Table of Contents

Introduction

Instant Reading Comprehension Practice provides short reading and writing exercises that develop and strengthen the skills needed for reading comprehension.

This book is divided into two main sections: *Comprehension Activities* and *Strategies in Writing*. *Comprehension Activities* is divided into eight sub-sections that focus specifically on each of the following comprehension skills:

- Finding Main Ideas
- Noting Details
- Using Context Clues
- Identifying Facts and Opinions

- Finding Cause and Effect
- Sequencing
- Making Inferences
- Predicting Outcomes

Each sub-section includes at least 30 passages with questions designed to challenge students and guide them towards mastery in one of the eight skill areas.

The *Strategies in Writing* section provides students with the opportunity to identify and practice the same comprehension skills but in an open-ended, short-answer format. The activities in this section allow students to focus on a specific strategy and to think more critically as they respond to a given writing task.

A teacher can

- choose to focus on one skill exclusively, going sequentially through the exercises.
- do a few exercises from each skill set to provide daily variety.
- assign specific exercises that will introduce, match, and/or strengthen strategies covered in the classroom.

Writing activities can be assigned at any time and in any order, but each activity focuses on a particular strategy. The strategy is noted at the top of the page. Each strategy has four activity pages, except for *Making Inferences* and *Predicting Outcomes*, which have three each.

Teaching Tips for Specific Exercises

You may want to go through one or two exercises together with the class.

At first, focus on critical-thinking skills rather than speed. Fluency and rate of reading will improve as students practice and gain confidence with each targeted skill.

Remind students that they should read EVERY answer choice. The first answer may sound correct, but there might be a better choice. If they can cross out just one wrong answer, they will have a much better chance of choosing the correct answer.

Finding Main Ideas

Students may find it helpful to sum up what they just read in a short sentence or two before reading the answer choices. Other students may find it helpful to first make a list of three or four key words from the text. Both strategies can help students focus on the most important parts of a passage and not be mislead by incorrect answer choices.

Remind students to choose an answer that covers most of whom or what the paragraph is about. Usually, wrong answers will focus either on details that are too small or too broad. For example, you may read a paragraph about three interesting things to see in California. Facts are given about the Golden Gate Bridge, a tree called Methuselah that is over 4,800 years old, and migrating gray whales off the coast. An answer that *only* talks about Methuselah is too "small" because it leaves out the bridge and the whales. An answer that talks about *all* the interesting things to see in California is too "big." The main idea is three interesting things from California, not *every* interesting thing. In other words, you should be thinking, "Not too big, not too small, but just right!"

Pick the correct answer. Students should think about what answer is too big, too small, just right . . . or just wrong!

The archer fish swims just under the surface of the water. When it spots a bug or spider hanging over the water from a twig or leaf, the archer fish spits! The archer fish spits so hard that it knocks the bug into the water and then gobbles it up!

What is the the main idea?

- **A.** Archer fish swim under the surface of the water when looking for food. (too small)
- **B.** Different kinds of fish eat different kinds of food. (too big)
- **C.** Archer fish have an unusual strategy for capturing food. (just right)

Noting Details

Remind students not to panic if they read a passage with a lot of details. They do not have to memorize or remember all the facts and figures! They can always go back and check the passage. Read the following example:

> Most of Earth is covered by oceans. The largest ocean is the Pacific Ocean. The second-largest ocean is the Atlantic Ocean. The third-largest ocean is the Indian Ocean.
>
> What is the second-largest ocean?
>
> **A.** Pacific Ocean
> **B.** Atlantic Ocean
> **C.** Indian Ocean
>
> *Answer: B*

Ask students if they had to memorize what they read to answer the question or if they went back and looked it up. Point out that all the information they need is still right in front of them and can be reread as many times as necessary.

Using Context Clues

Remind students not to stop reading! Reassure students that they are not expected to know what a word means or what word should go in the blank. They are solving a puzzle! They **must** finish reading the prompt. Then, they can reread the sentence while inserting one of the answer choices into the blank. Usually, they can eliminate choices because some answers will not make sense.

For example, no one expects a child to know the word *discombobulated* (confused, frustrated). Yet students can correctly choose it if they use the process of elimination, as seen in the following example:

> Jonah was _____ by all the bright lights, loud noises, and people rushing by.
>
> What word best completes the sentence?
>
> **A.** taught
> **B.** discombobulated
> **C.** lifted
>
> *Answer: B*

Point out that even if students couldn't understand the word *discombobulated*, they could cross out and eliminate *taught* and *lifted*. They could still get the right answer!

Identifying Facts and Opinions

Have students ask themselves, "Is this something I think, or do I know for certain?"

Riding a bike is more fun than roller-skating. If I **think** it, it is an **opinion**.

Some people like to ride bikes more than they like to roller-skate. If it is **certain** or if I can prove it, it is a **fact**.

Finding Cause and Effect

Have students ask themselves, "What happened, and why did it happen?"

What happened is the **effect**. **Why** it happened is the **cause**. If they forget this, students can write **What = Effect** and **Why = Cause** on the top of their page until the information can easily be recalled.

Example: When Lisa read the book, she learned that a giraffe's heart is two feet long.

What happened? (**effect**) Lisa learned something. Why did it happen? (**cause**) Lisa read a book.

Sequencing

Ask students to read over the sentences in the order they think the events happened. Think about what comes first and what comes later. Think about whether the order makes sense. Make sure the last sentence could not have happened until the previous ones did. Consider the following example:

> **1.** When her television turned on, Ms. Larson thought Scott was a genius.
>
> **2.** Ms. Larson's television set wasn't working.
>
> **3.** Ms. Larson didn't see Scott plug the cord into the electrical socket.
>
> What is the correct sequence?
> **A.** 1, 2, 3
> **B.** 3, 2, 1
> **C.** 2, 3, 1
> *Answer: C*

Making Inferences

When we make an inference, we use **clues** from the story to figure out something the author hasn't told us.

Example: Caesar's heart pounded! He felt a cold trickle of sweat run down his back.

Most likely, was Caesar hungry, tired, or afraid? If Caesar was hungry, he probably wouldn't be having such a strong physiological reaction. The same logic can be applied to being tired. Being afraid is the only logical answer.

Predicting Outcomes

When we predict an outcome, we make a logical guess about what is going to happen next. Remind students not to answer what happened. They should only be concerned about what might happen in the **future**.

Example: At the beach, Callie saw a sign that said, "No swimming. Dangerous currents."

Have students make logical guesses about what might happen next. (Callie stays out of the water; Callie goes into the water, and she gets caught in a dangerous current, etc.)

Remember: Insist that students read every answer choice! Have them eliminate or cross out the answer choices that don't make sense or that they know are wrong!

Name _Emme_   Date _8/5/2014_

Super-Sized

The ostrich egg is the largest egg of any living bird. An average ostrich egg is about six inches long and five inches wide. The egg weighs about three pounds. It would take about six times longer to hard-boil an ostrich egg than it would to hard-boil a chicken egg. Even though an ostrich egg is the largest of all bird eggs, it is the smallest egg relative to the size of the adult bird.

What is the main idea?

   A. An ostrich egg is about six inches long.
   B. An ostrich egg is the largest of all bird eggs.
   C. An ostrich egg weighs about three pounds.

Finding Balance

A balanced meal is made up of all the main food groups. The next time you eat, check that you have some fruits and vegetables, some proteins (like meat or beans), some grains (like rice or pasta), and some dairy (like cheese) on your plate. Try to avoid foods that have too much sugar, salt, or fat. Eating balanced meals every day can help to keep you healthy.

What is the main idea?

   A. Try to stay away from foods that have too much sugar, salt, or fat.
   B. Check to see that you have beans and cheese on your dinner plate.
   C. Eating meals made up of all the food groups every day can help to keep you healthy.

Name _Emmel_ Date _8 / 5 / 20 /4_

New Kid in Town

Jimmy was nervous about starting mid-year at a new school. He was new to the neighborhood and had not yet made any friends. After Jimmy got to school, the principal noticed that Jimmy was trying to find his classroom. "Good morning! You must be Jimmy," said the principal in a friendly voice. The principal showed Jimmy the way and introduced him to his teacher. Jimmy felt a lot better knowing he was welcome at the new school.

What is the main idea?
- **A.** Jimmy had moved from out of town with his parents and didn't have any friends.
- **B.** The principal helped Jimmy to feel more comfortable at his new school.
- **C.** Jimmy got lost at school trying to find his classroom.

The Appearance of Roy G. Biv

A rainbow is an arc of colors that appears in the sky when the sun shines through rain. It is seen opposite the sun. There are seven colors that appear in a rainbow. Starting from the outside of the arc, the colors are red, orange, yellow, green, blue, indigo, and violet. Many people remember the order of the colors by thinking of Roy G. Biv. Every letter in this "name" stands for a color.

What is the main idea?
- **A.** A rainbow is an arc of seven colors that appears in the sky when the sun shines through rain.
- **B.** A rainbow usually has seven colors.
- **C.** Roy G. Biv is not the name of a real person.

Name _____ **Date** _____

Special Scoops

Kim and her grandma go out for ice cream every year on Kim's birthday. Kim usually orders two scoops of vanilla ice cream topped with hot fudge and colorful sprinkles. This past birthday, Kim surprised her grandma. She ordered mint chocolate-chip ice cream, hot fudge, and gummy bears!

What is the main idea?

A. Kim always orders vanilla ice cream topped with hot fudge and sprinkles.

B. Kim and her grandma love eating ice cream.

C. Kim and her grandma go out for ice cream every year on Kim's birthday.

Legless Lizards

A glass snake is really a lizard without legs. This lizard can grow up to five feet long, although its tail makes up two-thirds of its body. In other words, the tail of an adult glass snake is a bit over three feet long. It gets its name because of what it can do to its tail. When the lizard feels it is in danger, it can break its tail at all or most of its joints. The tail shatters like glass, and the little pieces then wriggle on their own for several minutes. This gives the body of the lizard time to get away.

What is the main idea?

A. Glass snakes can shed their tails when they feel they are in danger.

B. Everything that is called a snake is not always a snake.

C. The glass snake's tail is two-thirds of its body.

Name _____ **Date** _____

Delicious Mix

An Arnold Palmer is a drink many people enjoy. It is made by mixing equal parts of lemonade and iced tea. People can order Arnold Palmers at many restaurants, or they can mix their own at home. Arnold Palmers are even sold ready to drink at some grocery stores. People who like to drink Arnold Palmers can have them nearly anywhere they go.

What is the main idea?

   A. An Arnold Palmer is made with equal parts of lemonade and iced tea.
   B. Drinks called "Arnold Palmers" are popular and easy to make or buy.
   C. People can order an Arnold Palmer at most restaurants.

First-Day Friends

Marco moved to the United States from another country. He didn't speak English very well and was nervous on his first day at his new school. Marco met a boy named Ralph while walking to school. Ralph was able to communicate with Marco enough for Marco to learn where everything was at school. Marco was very thankful to have made a new friend.

What is the main idea?

   A. Marco was nervous when he walked to school for the first time.
   B. Marco and Ralph were cousins who went to the same school.
   C. Marco didn't speak English well but was able to learn where things were at school thanks to a new friend.

Name _____   **Date** _____

Sparky the Dog

One morning, a magic fairy paid a visit to Sparky the Dog. The fairy touched the dog's nose with her wand and granted him the ability to talk. When Sparky's owners came outside, Sparky said, "Good morning, Mr. and Mrs. Wills!" They couldn't believe their ears! Sparky went on to tell them how much he loved walking with them and that he didn't like the new food they had been feeding him. The Wills family loved its talking dog and had him translate all the neighborhood dogs' likes and dislikes for their owners.

What is the main idea?
A. Sparky became very popular with the other dogs after he learned how to speak to humans.
B. Sparky was magically able to talk and translate for other dogs who lived in the neighborhood.
C. Sparky was magically able to change the food he didn't like into food he liked.

Cleaning Lessons

Ann's sister keeps messing up the room they share, no matter how much Ann asks her to be neat. Ann realizes that her sister has never learned how to be neat, so Ann gives her sister lessons. After each lesson, Ann gives her sister a sticker. One day, Ann comes home and finds that her sister has cleaned up the entire room. There is only one little mess on the floor—where her sister is putting all her stickers into a scrapbook.

What is the main idea?
A. Ann teaches her sister how to be neat, and her sister cleans their room.
B. Ann's sister keeps messing up their room, so Ann asks her mom if she can have her own room.
C. Ann's sister keeps messing up their room with stickers and scrapbooks.

Name _____ **Date** _____

Vegetable Victory

Laura and Vern wanted to plant a vegetable garden in their back yard, but the soil in their yard was full of rocks. The two then bought a book on how to create their own soil in a raised planter bed. Laura and Vern followed the book's instructions on how to build a planter box. Then, they layered hay, fertilizer, straw, and compost. Afterwards, they planted seeds and then watered the garden every day. Now, their garden grows wonderfully.

What is the main idea?

   A. Laura and Vern made a vegetable garden in a raised planter bed, and it worked wonderfully.
   B. The soil in Laura and Vern's back yard was not good for growing vegetables.
   C. Vegetable seeds need to be watered every day in order to grow.

Fast Wheels

When Kare Adenegan was only twelve years old, she was the fifth-fastest wheelchair sprinter in the world. Kare has gone 100 meters in just over 20 seconds. When Kare was younger, her parents wouldn't let her play sports. They didn't think Kare could because she was disabled. During the 2012 Paralympic Games, Kare saw athletes who didn't let their disabilities stop themselves from competing. Kare knew then that nothing was going to stop her. She trains twice a week and still finds time to finish her homework. She said, "I want to be able to reach out and say to people, 'You can have a go at this; you can't just give up.'"

What is the main idea?

   A. Many disabled people are not allowed to play sports.
   B. Kare Adenegan watched the 2012 Paralympic Games.
   C. Kare Adenegan is a determined wheelchair sprinter.

Name _____ **Date** _____

Eight Seconds

Bull riding is a very dangerous rodeo event. It involves a person trying to stay on a large bull while the bull tries to buck that person off. Riders are only allowed to hold on to a rope with one hand. To complete a ride, the rider must stay on the bull for eight seconds. With one stomp or kick, these massive animals can seriously injure a person. Some riders wear helmets, but many just wear cowboy hats.

What is the main idea?

  A. Riders are only allowed to hold on to the rope with one hand.
  B. Bull riding is a very dangerous rodeo event.
  C. Riders try to stay on the bull for eight seconds.

Love Your Planet

Earth Day is on April 22. It is a reminder for people to conserve our planet's resources. Whenever possible, we should recycle paper, plastic, glass, and metal. We should also reuse older items before buying new ones and avoid using plastic when we don't need it. Earth Day is the perfect time to establish new habits that are good for the planet.

What is the main idea?

  A. People should not celebrate Earth Day every day.
  B. People should not use plastic items on a daily basis.
  C. Earth Day is a day to remember to conserve Earth's resources.

Name _____   **Date** _____

Rocket Man

The students took one look at their teacher and knew it was going to be a good day. He was wearing a silly rocket hat that had streamers hanging down the side. The last time he wore a silly hat, they did a fun project in class. After everyone was seated, he announced, "Today we are going to learn about astronauts and build model rockets." The students were so excited that they cheered with joy.

What is the main idea?

A. The students were excited about what was planned for the day.
B. The students laughed at the teacher's silly hat.
C. The teacher's silly hat was a clue that they were going to have a party.

Backyard Bounty

Bill's family loves eating salad with dinner. Every evening, Bill goes to the garden in his back yard. He picks fresh lettuce and tomatoes. He washes the vegetables and cuts them up to make a salad. Because he has a garden, Bill does not have to go to the grocery store very often.

What is the main idea?

A. Bill grows a vegetable garden because his family has a large back yard.
B. Bill's family must have salad with every dinner.
C. Bill doesn't have to buy salad for his family because he has a vegetable garden.

Name _____ **Date** _____

Surf's Up

Brad caught the biggest wave of the day and sped down the mountain of water. On his surfboard, the wave looked as if it was going to curl over, so he set himself up to ride inside the tube. The lip of the wave curled around him as he glided effortlessly on the surface. As the tube was closing, he rode out just before the whitewater covered him. Brad smiled and turned around to paddle out for another ride.

What is the main idea?

A. The wave crashed on Brad, making him unable to complete the ride.

B. In a surfing contest, Brad caught the biggest wave of the day.

C. Brad caught a great ride on his surfboard, and that made him want to ride again.

In the Clouds

Belle said, "I live in a little town. Only 30,000 people live in my town. Everything in my town is close to the ground. The tallest building is only three stories tall. The Burj Khalifa is a skyscraper. It is in Dubai. Dubai is a city in the United Arab Emirates. The skyscraper is only one building, but 35,000 people can fit in it at one time! That is more people than live in my entire town! The skyscraper has 2,909 steps. They go from the first floor to the 160th floor. I think that might be more steps than in my entire town! The building has 62 miles of water pipes, and an average of 250,000 gallons of water runs through the pipes every day. I think the Burj Khalifa is like a town that rises into the sky!"

What is the main idea?

A. There are differences between Belle's town and a skyscraper in Dubai.

B. Belle would like to live in a town that rises into the sky.

C. More people can fit in the Burj Khalifa skyscraper than there are in Belle's town.

Name _____ **Date** _____

Tower 32

Kate was excited about her first day as a lifeguard. She was assigned to tower 32 at Sunset Beach. Worried about other people's ocean safety, she carefully watched the swimmers. When Kate's shift was over, the next lifeguard came to replace her. He asked Kate how her day was. She replied, "Just how I wanted it—the swimmers were all safe and injury-free."

What is the main idea?
- **A.** Kate's first day as a lifeguard was good because all the swimmers were safe.
- **B.** At the beach, Kate was too nervous to focus on the swimmers.
- **C.** Kate asked for a replacement lifeguard to come because she was so nervous.

Stuffed Pig

From the time Ben was seven, any time someone gave him money, he saved half of it in a piggy bank. He used the other half of the gift money to buy new toys and clothes. Ben's brother Rob didn't like the idea of only getting to spend half, so Rob always spent all his gift money. By the time Ben was twelve, he had three hundred dollars in his piggy bank. That was just enough to buy a brand-new bike—and to make Rob jealous.

What is the main idea?
- **A.** Rob was jealous that Ben always got more gift money than he did.
- **B.** Ben was able to buy a bike because for five years he had saved half of his gift money.
- **C.** Ben took a class that taught him how to both save and spend money wisely.

Name _____ **Date** _____

Birthday Wishes

Sophia was really looking forward to getting her birthday presents after the family dinner. She was hoping to get a new puppy from her parents. All summer, Sophia had been talking about wanting one. To show she could take care of it, she had taken care of the neighbors' dogs when her neighbors weren't home. Sophia walked the dogs, fed them, and even cleaned up after them. After dinner, Sophia first opened up a package of socks. Then she opened up a package with a new toothbrush. Sophia said, "Thank you" and tried to look pleased. Then her brother came in holding a puppy. Sophia's eyes shimmered with happiness.

What is the main idea?

 A. Sophia took care of the neighbors' dogs.
B. Sophia was pleased with the first gifts she opened.
C. Sophia got what she wanted for her birthday.

Ironman

An Ironman Triathlon is a grueling race consisting of three events. First, the athlete must swim 2.4 miles. Second, he or she must bike for 112 miles. Third is a marathon run—that's 26.2 miles! All this is done on the same day without a break in between events. People who compete in an Ironman race must train regularly to build up their endurance.

What is the main idea?

A. Athletes may finish the three events of the Ironman Triathlon on separate days.
B. An Ironman Triathlon is a competition of swimming, biking, and running.
C. Those who compete in an Ironman race must build up endurance.

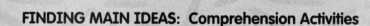

Name _____   **Date** _____

Aiming for the Stars

Ned dreamed of one day flying a rocket ship into outer space. As a child, he built model rockets, studied pilots, and loved watching sci-fi movies. When he was only eight years old, Ned made it his goal to go on a space mission once he grew up. He worked hard to reach his goals, and eventually, he became an astronaut. Ned described his first trip into space as "unreal" because he couldn't believe it was really happening.

What is the main idea?

A. Ned's trip to space was not real because it was just a dream.
B. Ned dreamed of one day flying a rocket ship into outer space.
C. Ned worked hard and achieved his goal of one day going into space.

Hot Water

Dominica is an island in the Caribbean. There is a lake in Dominica that you can't drive to. It is about eight miles from the closest road. To get to the lake, you have to cross sulfur springs. You have to go over mountains and through gorges. You can't swim in or drink the water from the lake. The water in the lake is so hot that it is boiling. Dominica is a volcanic island. The lake is over a fumarole. A fumarole is an opening in the planet's crust. Fumaroles are often in the same areas as volcanoes. Heat from inside Earth makes the water boil. Only one man has ever crossed the boiling lake from above. The man crossed over ropes suspended in the air so that he could film the lake from above.

What is the main idea?

A. A fumarole has created a boiling lake on the island of Dominica.
B. Dominica is an island in the Caribbean that people should go to see.
C. Crossing over a boiling lake on suspended ropes is very dangerous and foolish.

Name _____ **Date** _____

Thick Skin

Claire won the grand prize at her school for reading the most books within the school year. The grand prize was a trip to Marine Life Zoo, where the winner would assist a zookeeper. Claire chose to help care for the dolphins. Claire fed the dolphins fish. When she felt one dolphin's skin, she thought that it felt like rubber. The trainer told Claire that a dolphin's surface layer of skin is ten times thicker than the skin of any mammal that lives on land. The trainer also told Claire that every two to four hours, the whole top layer of a dolphin's skin sloughs off. This means that dead cells are replaced by new ones nine times faster than humans!

What is the main idea?

A. At Marine Life Zoo, Claire read a book about dolphin skin.

B. At Marine Life Zoo, Claire learned about dolphin skin while assisting a zookeeper.

C. A dolphin's outer skin layer is ten times thicker than Claire's.

Icy Inspiration

During a trip to the Arctic, Clarence Birdseye watched native people freeze fish on the ice. He saw that this fast method of freezing did no damage to the flesh of the fish. The method left the fish tasting almost the same as fresh fish. Birdseye went home and did some experiments with different kinds of freezing devices. That was the start of the modern-day frozen-food business.

What is the main idea?

A. Freezing fish on the ice does no damage to the flesh of the fish.

B. Birdseye started the modern-day frozen-food business after watching the way native people froze fish.

C. Birdseye experimented with different kinds of freezing devices.

Name _____   Date _____

Kindness Matters

Mira goes to Carl's Candy Shop every day after school and buys one piece of licorice. One day, Mira found a wallet on the floor of the shop and quickly gave it to the store clerk. Minutes later, a man rushed into the candy store and asked if anyone had turned in a wallet. After the man described his wallet, the clerk gave him the wallet Mira had found. The man was very relieved. He offered to give Mira a reward, but Mira said she only did what was right. The man said, "One day, your kindness will come back to you."

answer A
What is the main idea?
- **A.** A man was able to get his wallet back after Mira did the right thing.
- **B.** Mira was given a reward for turning in a lost wallet.
- **C.** Mira found a lost wallet when she was buying a package of licorice.

Open for Business

Everyone in town was excited. A new theater was opening its doors for business. For one night only, all the city residents could watch a movie at half-price. The lines were very long. It seemed as if everyone in the entire city hoped to take advantage of the half-price ticket offer.

What is the main idea?
- **A.** On opening night, many city residents were excited to watch a half-price movie.
- **B.** The new theater was opening its doors for business.
- **C.** More people go to theaters when tickets are offered at half-price.

Name _____   Date _____

Olympic Greatness

The Olympic Games is a worldwide event. There are both Summer and Winter Games. Every two years, the Summer and Winter Games alternate. The games are held in different countries each time. The Olympic flag has five rings. The rings are blue, yellow, black, green, and red. Every national flag in the world has at least one of those colors. Thousands of athletes from across the globe compete in a variety of events. For each event, medals are given to the top three athletes or teams. The Olympic Games are considered by most to be the greatest sports competition.

What is the main idea?

A. For each event, medals are given to the top three athletes or teams.

B. The Olympic Games is a worldwide event with both summer and winter sports.

C. The Olympic Games has its own flag.

Favorite Riddles

Emma was writing down a list of her favorite riddles to share with Jake. She wrote, "What goes up and never comes down?" Then she wrote, "What kind of coat can be put on only when wet?" Next she wrote, "With no protection, a man went outside in the pouring rain, but not a hair on his head got wet. How come?" Emma wrote the answers on the back of the page, but Jake already knew the answers. "Your age, paint, and because he was bald," he said. Emma then asked Jake, "For my next riddle, should I write 'The yolk of the egg *are* white,' or 'The yolk of the egg *is* white?'" Jake started to laugh. "You can't fool me," he said. "I know that egg yolks are yellow!"

What is the main idea?

A. Emma didn't know that egg yolks are yellow.

B. Emma wrote three riddles on one side of a piece of paper and the answers on the back.

C. Emma was writing down her favorite riddles to share with her friend.

Name _____   **Date** _____

Center of the States

Betty has lived in Lebanon, Kansas her whole life. Betty likes where she lives because Lebanon is the geographical center of the United States. This is only accurate, however, if you just count the 48 states that touch. If you include Alaska and Hawaii, the geographic center moves to Belle Fourche, South Dakota. Betty has never been to a beach. Next July, Betty and her family are going on a two-week vacation. They are flying to Miami, Florida. They will stay on the beach. Betty can't wait to play in the waves and to build sandcastles.

When is Betty going on vacation?
  A. next June
  B. next July
  C. next August

Fresh Fruit

Noah and his family love to eat fruit. They decided to start their own fruit garden. They first planted cantaloupe, watermelon, and strawberry seeds. Then Noah's dad decided to plant an orange tree. The entire family enjoyed having fresh fruit right from their back yard.

What was one of the first fruits Noah and his family planted?
  A. watermelon
  B. oranges
  C. blueberries

Name _____ **Date** _____

Early Riser

Madison wakes up at 6:30 every morning. She eats a healthy breakfast after she gets dressed. If the weather is nice, Madison walks with her mom to school. Madison is usually at school by 7:45 a.m.

What time does Madison wake up?

  A. 7:45 a.m.

  B. 6:30 a.m.

  C. 6:45 a.m.

Giving Thanks

The Yoshira family is moving to a new house. They were packing their things in boxes on Saturday. Rick, their friend and neighbor, came over that day to help them pack. To show her appreciation, Mrs. Yoshira gave Rick a $20 gift card to his favorite restaurant.

Who gave Rick a gift?

  A. Mr. Yoshira

  B. Rick's boss

  C. Mrs. Yoshira

Name _____ **Date** _____

Borrowed Books

Public libraries let people borrow books, music, and movies for free. They let people use computers, too. Returning books and other materials on time is important because others may want to borrow them. The borrowed items must be returned by a specified due date. If not, you will be charged a late fee. You should always bring back books and other borrowed items on time.

Why is returning books on time important?

A. If you don't, you will get a ticket.
B. If you don't, you will not get to check out more books.
C. Others may want to borrow them.

Tuvalu

Is your city larger than a country? Tuvalu is one of the world's smallest countries. It is only nine square miles. It is made up of nine tiny islands. Five of the islands are coral atolls, and the other four are undersea mountains that rise from the ocean floor. All the islands are low-lying. None of the islands have elevations over 15 feet above sea level! Tuvalu is in the Pacific Ocean. It is midway between Australia and Hawaii. It is a country without a single stream or river. People drink rainwater in order to survive. Tuvalu didn't become independent until 1978. Only about 12,000 people live in Tuvalu. Many small towns have more people than the entire country of Tuvalu!

Where do people get their drinking water on Tuvalu?

A. from streams
B. from rain
C. from rivers

Name _____ **Date** _____

Tax Not Included

Robin and her mother were shopping for new school clothes. They went to a department store that was having a huge sale. The store sold a large assortment of toys, housewares, and clothes. Robin was told that she could spend no more than $40. Robin picked out new jeans that cost $25. She found a shirt she liked for $15. Then Robin remembered that with sales tax, the total would be more than $40.

What were Robin and her mother shopping for?
  A. play clothes
  B. doll clothes
  C. school clothes

Bake Me a Cake

Manuel and his mom were baking a special dessert. They started by mixing all the dry ingredients in a large bowl. Manuel and his mom mixed the wet ingredients in a separate, smaller bowl. They poured the wet mixture on top of the dry mixture and mixed everything together. Then the new mixture was ready to pour into the pan and bake.

What did Manuel and his mom mix in the smaller bowl?
  A. the wet ingredients
  B. the dry ingredients
  C. all the ingredients

Name _____ **Date** _____

Lost in Translation

Riley's family went to the zoo. An elephant had just been born there. Its name was Simba. It weighed 250 pounds at birth. Riley thought the elephant should have been named "Tembo" instead of "Simba." That's because in Swahili, "tembo" means elephant while "simba" means lion! Regardless of its name, Riley was very excited to see the baby elephant. She was hoping to get close-up pictures of it.

How much did Simba weigh at birth?

A. 250 pounds
B. 520 pounds
C. 5200 pounds

Out with the Old

An old warehouse building is being torn down. A new community library will be built in its place. The library will be two stories tall. Children's books and magazines will be on the first floor. Research materials and computer stations will be on the second floor.

Where will the research materials be located?

A. on the first floor
B. on the second floor
C. next to the children's books

Name _____ **Date** _____

Fierce Fish

Did you know that sharks don't have any bones? Shark skeletons are not like human skeletons. Shark skeletons are made of cartilage. Cartilage is a strong, flexible material. Humans have cartilage in their noses and outer ears. Sharks have a better sense of smell than any other fish. Like humans, sharks have large hearts with four separate chambers.

What are shark skeletons made of?

A. bone

B. chambers

C. cartilage

Different but United

The United States of America is made up of 50 states. Which one is the smallest? Which one is the biggest? The smallest state is Rhode Island. The largest state is Alaska. Nearly 500 Rhode Islands can fit in Alaska! Rhode Island was the 13th state to enter the Union. It joined on May 29, 1790. Alaska was the 49th state to enter the Union. It joined on January 3, 1959. Every state has a state flower. Rhode Island's state flower is the violet. Alaska's state flower is the forget-me-not.

What state has the violet as its state flower?

A. the 13th state

B. the largest state

C. the state that joined on January 3, 1959

A+

Name _____   **Date** _____

Leap Day

Dawn was born on Leap Day. Leap Day is February 29. Usually, February only has 28 days. Every four years, an extra day is added to the month. When that happens, it is called a Leap Year, and the extra day is called a Leap Day. Sometimes, Dawn celebrates her birthday on February 28. Sometimes, she celebrates on March 1. Dawn has a big birthday party every four years.

2004

FEBRUARY					2004	
SUN	MON	TUE	WED	THU	FRI	SAT
		1	2	3	4	5
6	7	8	9	10	11	12
13	14	15	16	17	18	19
20	21	22	23	24	25	26
27	28					

On what day was Dawn born?

A. March 1

B. February 28

C. February 29

Game Night

Greg's family likes to play a game together. The game is a video game that asks questions just like on a TV game show. Greg uses the game controller to select questions. Everyone in his family shouts out answers to the questions.

What does Greg's family like to play together?

A. a card game

B. a board game

C. a video game

Name _____ Date _____

Family Night Out

Sara's family goes out to dinner every Friday night. They go to the same restaurant each time. It is everyone's favorite restaurant. Sara's brother, Levi, always orders the same meal. Levi says that he loves it too much not to order it. After dinner, Sara and her family take a walk around the block. They always go past a pet store. Sara likes to look at the puppies in the window, while Levi likes to look at the kittens.

When does the family go out to dinner?

 A. every Friday
B. every night
C. every other Friday

Summer Down Under

Cameron and his family went on vacation in December. They each packed T-shirts, shorts, and bathing suits. They flew to Australia, where it was summer, and stayed for two weeks. Cameron and his family planned on hiking around the base of Uluru. Uluru is a huge rock, and the hike around it is almost six miles long. Cameron wanted to see the rock at dawn and dusk. He had read that during those times, the rock appears a glowing red.

What did Cameron and his family pack?

A. winter coats
B. bathing suits
C. hiking boots

Name _____ **Date** _____

Writing a Letter

To mail a letter, you have to address the envelope in a certain way. In the middle of the envelope, write the name and address of the person to whom you are mailing it. Write your name and address (return address) in the top-left corner. Place a postage stamp in the top-right corner. Some people feel email will replace this type of letter writing. When you email a letter, all you have to do is press the "send" button. Of course, you also need to have a computer and an Internet connection!

Where does the postage stamp go on an envelope?

A. in the top-left corner
B. in the top-right corner
C. in the middle

The Sleeping One

Don't expect to see a Common Poorwill during the winter. This bird survives the cold by going into a dormant, or sleeping, state. Its heart rate and breathing rate drops down to almost nothing. Its body temperature can drop from 106°F to 43°F. It takes about seven hours for the bird to wake up out of hibernation. Native Americans of the Hopi tribe knew this bird as *Holchko*. In the Hopi language, *Holchko* means "the sleeping one." Scientists didn't discover until 1946 that the Common Poorwill went into this dormant state. Before that, they were unaware that birds could be dormant for so long.

Native Americans of what tribe knew the Common Poorwill as *Holchko*?

A. Hopi
B. Yaqui
C. Yuma

Name _____ **Date** _____

Faith's Flute

Faith practices her flute every night after dinner. Most nights, Faith practices for about half an hour. Faith's teacher thinks Faith should practice ten additional minutes every day. Faith's parents agree with her teacher. Faith thinks that if she practices for forty minutes, she should not have to clear the table after dinner.

About how long does Faith practice now?

  A. 10 minutes

  B. 30 minutes

  C. 40 minutes

Palomino Party

Maya's parents gave her a horse-themed party for her birthday. The party was at a nearby horse stable. Everyone was able to have a turn riding on a horse. The horse was a palomino mare named "Star." A mare is a female horse. A palomino is a lighter-colored horse ranging from a pale cream to a deep, rich golden color. Maya's cake was even decorated with a few toy horses, one of which was a palomino.

What is true about the cake?

  A. It was shaped like a horse.

  B. It had a picture of a palomino horse on it.

  C. It had toy horses on top.

A X

Name _____ **Date** _____

State Reports

Henry's class was assigned to write state reports. Mr. Martinez wrote each state abbreviation on a little piece of paper. He put the papers in a brown bag for the students to choose from. Without looking, Henry grabbed a paper that said "MT." Henry plans on going to the library after school to check out books on Montana. Henry was glad he picked "MT" instead of "ME," "MD," or "MA." He didn't want to write about Maine, Maryland, or Massachusetts. He thought a western state would be more interesting than an eastern one.

Where is Henry going after school?
A. to a western state
B. to the library
C. to the bookstore

Larry Legend

Larry Bird is a retired NBA basketball player. Many people think he was one of the greatest basketball players of all time. Bird played for the Boston Celtics his entire career. He won three NBA championships. One time, during the 1986 NBA All-Star Weekend, Bird was getting ready to participate in a three-point shooting contest. Bird walked into the locker room, looked around, and didn't say a word. Finally he said, "I want all of you to know I am winning this thing. I'm just looking around to see who's gonna finish up second." What happened? Bird won the shooting contest.

Which basketball team did Larry Bird play for?
A. Boston Celtics
B. Boston Cardinals
C. Baltimore Celtics

Name _____ **Date** _____

Take a Picture

Many special cameras can take pictures in or under water. People often use these special cameras to take pictures of sea life. They may take pictures of the blue-ringed octopus. The blue-ringed octopus has bright blue rings on it. It may be pretty, but it has a poisonous bite. People may take pictures of dangerous sharks, but only if the photographers are safely protected in a shark cage! Sometimes people may just take pictures of friends while they swim.

Who uses underwater cameras most often?
A. people in shark cages
B. people swimming with friends
C. The story does not say.

Big Babies

Is it possible for a baby to be larger than its parent? Before answering, one should think about a particular species of frog called the "paradoxical frog." It lives in South America. The adult frog grows to be only $2\frac{1}{4}$ to $2\frac{1}{2}$ inches long, yet the tadpole grows to a length of $6\frac{1}{2}$ inches! The big tadpole then shrinks down into an adult. To become an adult, it shrinks down to a third of its original body size! For many years, scientists did not know that the tadpole and the frog belonged to the same species.

Where does the paradoxical frog live?
A. South America
B. North America
C. Central America

Name _____   Date _____

Read Across America Day

March 2 is the birthday of children's author Dr. Seuss. Since 1998, March 2nd has also been known as "Read Across America Day." On this day, people across the country celebrate reading. They honor Dr. Seuss on this day by reading books to children. Dr. Seuss wrote *The Cat in the Hat*. He also wrote *Green Eggs and Ham* and *Horton Hatches the Egg*. Dr. Seuss's first published book was *And To Think That I Saw It On Mulberry Street*. Good thing Dr. Seuss didn't give up easily because that book was turned down 27 times!

When is Read Across America Day?
- **A.** May 2
- **B.** March 2
- **C.** March 22

A Lot of Water

Lake Tahoe is a very large lake. It is located along the border between California and Nevada. About two-thirds of its shoreline is in California. It is the second-deepest lake in the United States. The deepest lake in the United States is in Oregon. Lake Tahoe is the sixteenth-deepest lake in the world. Its deepest point is 1,645 feet. There is a lot of water in Lake Tahoe. If it were poured out, it could cover a flat area the size of California and still be 14 inches deep!

Where is Lake Tahoe located?
- **A.** between California and Arizona
- **B.** between California and Nevada
- **C.** between California and Oregon

Name _____ **Date** _____

Counting Steps

A pedometer is a device that counts each step a person takes. People often wear pedometers on their belts or wrists. Most pedometers work by counting electronic pulses each time a person takes a step. The number of steps multiplied by the person's step length equals the distance he or she has walked all day.

Where do people often wear pedometers?
  A. on their shoes
  B. on their shoulders
  C. on their belts

Family Menu

For dinner on Friday, the family ate pasta and salad. They did not finish it all. For lunch on Saturday, the family had homemade tacos. The tacos were made with beef and onions. The tacos were then topped with lettuce and tomatoes. For Sunday's dinner, the family all shared the leftovers from the previous two days.

What did the family eat for dinner on Friday?
  A. salad
  B. leftovers
  C. tacos

Name _____ **Date** _____

BASE Jumping

What is BASE jumping? The name comes from different places people can jump from: a <u>b</u>uilding, <u>a</u>ntenna, <u>s</u>pan, and <u>E</u>arth. (A bridge would be a span. A cliff would be Earth.) BASE jumping is not for everybody. In BASE jumping, people jump from a fixed object. A person uses a parachute to break his or her fall. Two men BASE-jumped off of the Burj Khalifa skyscraper in Dubai, United Arab Emirates. They jumped from the 160th floor. They dropped at a speed of 140 miles per hour. The jump took them 90 seconds. They had only ten seconds to open their parachutes.

A BASE jumper might jump from .

A. Air Force One, the president's plane.

B. a rescue helicopter.

C. the Empire State Building.

Desert Survivors

Camels are better adapted to life in the desert than almost any other mammal. For example, camels are the only mammals that do not have round red blood cells. <u>Their red blood cells are elliptical.</u> This oval shape helps the cells to move even when a camel's blood thickens. (When one does not get much water, one's blood will thicken.) People often talk about how the pioneers used cow pies, or dried cow waste, as fuel for their campfires in the United States. Camel dung doesn't have to be dried out. It comes out so dry that it can be used as fuel as soon as it leaves the animal!

What is true about a camel's red blood cells?

A. They are elliptical.

B. They are thick.

C. They are round.

Name _____ **Date** _____

Generous Donation

It had been two years since Monica had last cut her hair. It had grown down to the bottom of her back. Monica was finally ready for a haircut, so she asked her mom if she would take her to the hair salon. When Monica's mom took her, the hairdresser told Monica that if she cut off ten inches, she could donate her hair. It could be made into a wig and given to someone who had lost his or her hair. After her haircut, Monica was doubly pleased with the <u>outcome</u>. She looked great, and she had helped a stranger.

Which word can best replace the underlined word?
 A. result
   B. scissors
   C. picture

Memorizing Moves

Mrs. Alvarez is the best dance teacher in the world. She always <u>demonstrates</u> each difficult dance move before we try it by ourselves. She first does it slowly, and then she repeats the move several times until everyone has it memorized. Everyone in my class likes her.

The underlined word means
   A. carries.
   B. builds.
 C. shows.

Name _____ **Date** _____

Homework First

Because Chad and Emily weren't finished with their homework, they had to work on it while their cousins were visiting for the day. It was very hard for them to concentrate. Every ten minutes, they got up to see what their cousins were doing. Chad and Emily found that they just couldn't sit still.

Which word can best replace the underlined word?
- **A.** sleep
- **B.** focus
- **C.** play

Foul Ball

My dad took me to watch a professional baseball game. I was excited when I caught a foul ball in the third inning. I put the ball in my backpack for the remainder of the game. I didn't take it out until the game was over.

Which word can best replace the underlined word?
- **A.** play
- **B.** rest
- **C.** beginning

Name _____ **Date** _____

Jeans

Isaiah has seven pairs of blue jeans and one pair of black jeans. There is a very good chance that he will wear blue jeans tomorrow. In fact, the <u>likelihood</u> that he will wear blue jeans is seven out of eight.

Which word can best replace the underlined word?

A. reason
B. fact
C. probability

Wacky Weather

On January 22, 1943, at 7:30 a.m., the temperature in Spearfish, South Dakota was a chilly ˉ4°F. In just two minutes, the temperature shot up to 45°F! It went up 49 degrees in just two minutes! By 9:00 a.m. the temperature was 54°F. Then, it <u>plummeted</u>. In just 27 minutes, it went back down to ˉ4°F! The National Weather Service said it was ". . . likely due to cold air and warm air sloshing back and forth along the plains at the base of the Black Hills."

Which word can best replace the underlined word?

A. dropped
B. increased
C. placed

Name _____ **Date** _____

What Does It Say?

Tracy takes her time when she writes. She makes sure that whoever reads her writing will not have to question what letters he or she is looking at. Tracy's sister Gabriella does the opposite. She rushes when she writes, and it always looks sloppy. Tracy's writing is much more <u>legible</u>.

The underlined word means

  A. easy to write.

  (**B.**) easy to read.

  C. easy to see.

Tough Question

Cody asked Braden a difficult math question that Braden didn't know how to answer. Braden asked Cody to <u>simplify</u> the question so that it would not be so hard to understand. When Cody asked Braden the second time, Braden knew exactly what Cody was asking about. Braden was then able to show Cody how he could solve the question himself.

The underlined word means

  A. make harder.

  B. make softer.

  (**C.**) make easier.

Name _____ **Date** _____

Picky Eater

Gina was babysitting a baby boy. She was feeding the baby some applesauce for his breakfast. Every time Gina gave the baby a spoonful, he would spit it out. After ten or more tries, Gina offered the baby an <u>alternative</u> food. She gave him pancakes instead. The baby was much happier eating the pancakes.

The underlined word means

  A. easier.
  B. different.
  C. fresh.

Wild Animal

Randy the Raccoon was having a rough day. For some reason, he wasn't acting like himself. Usually, he is friendly to others, but he wasn't nice at lunchtime today. Randy showed bad <u>conduct</u> in the school cafeteria when he yelled and threw his food at the other raccoons. The cafeteria raccoon said, "You shouldn't waste food. Think of all the hungry mice that would be happy to eat it."

Which word can best replace the underlined word?
  A. behavior
  B. movies
  C. vegetables

Name _____ **Date** _____

Wobbly Legs

Our dinner table is very old and has become wobbly because one of the table's legs is loose. Last night during dinner, the weak leg broke off! Everything on the table slid a bit to the right! I stopped the bread from sliding onto the floor! My dad used a chair and some books to <u>support</u> the table so that we could finish eating. Tomorrow, we will likely go shopping for a new table.

The underlined word means
A. hold up.
B. look up.
C. break up.

Shark Food

The diver set out to <u>salvage</u> what he could from the sunken pirate ship. He had just discovered a small box that he was hoping was filled with gold pieces when he looked up and saw a huge shark. The shark was swimming directly towards him! The diver quickly picked up the small box and heaved it into the shark's open mouth! The shark swallowed the entire box, but then it turned around and swam away. When the diver got to the surface, he thought, "I'll take saving my life any day over being a shark's lunch. Still, I do wonder what was in that little box!"

The underlined word means
A. to feed.
B. to throw.
C. to save.

Name _____   **Date** _____

Zoo Trip

Grandpa and I were having a <u>conversation</u> about what we liked best from our trip to the zoo. Grandpa said that seeing the lions spend time with their new cubs was his favorite part. I said that feeding the ducks was my favorite part. We both want to go back again to see the monkeys.

Which word can best replace the underlined word?
- **A.** snack
- **B.** fight
- **C.** talk

Pool Play

Jill and Travis were playing with different objects that were in their pool. They wanted to see which things would sink or float. Travis loved diving down to get the objects that sank to the bottom of the pool. When Jill grabbed a coconut to throw into the pool, Travis was sure he'd be diving down to get it. Travis was very surprised when the coconut turned out to be <u>buoyant</u>.

The underlined word means
- **A.** able to float.
- **B.** quick to sink.
- **C.** hard and heavy.

Name _____   Date _____

Well-Prepared

Amy's teacher gave the entire class notes so that the students could study for the upcoming science test. Amy studied her notes every night after dinner. The night before the test, Amy's mom quizzed her, and Amy answered everything correctly. Amy felt <u>confident</u> that she was going to do a great job on the test.

The underlined word means
- **A.** wrong.
- **B.** bad.
- **C.** sure.

Spider Snacks

Jack and Tina had just finished making spider cupcakes. They had frosted the cupcakes with brown frosting and used thin red licorice to make eight legs on each cupcake. The most common number of eyes a spider has is eight, so they used eight small candies on each cupcake for the spider's eyes. When their friends came over, Jack and Tina asked them if they wanted a spider. At first their friends <u>declined</u>, but then when they saw the cupcake spiders, they changed their minds!

The underlined word means
- **A.** begged.
- **B.** refused.
- **C.** agreed.

Name _____   **Date** _____

Learning about Lincoln

Jerod had to write a report about Abe Lincoln. To get information, Jerod looked in books. He also looked on the Internet. In his notes, Jerod only wrote down the <u>significant</u> events from Lincoln's life. He knew that he didn't need to include in his notes the little details from Abe Lincoln's life. Instead, he needed to talk about what Lincoln did as president. He decided to delete the sentence about Lincoln liking rice pudding.

Which word can best replace the underlined word?

  A. important
  B. uninteresting
  C. childhood

Spider on the Loose

A tarantula had gotten out of its cage! All the students were nervous. When Troy spotted it on his chair, many students screeched. Some even started to run out of the room. Ms. Arachnid, the teacher, kept her <u>composure</u>. She very calmly put out her hand. When the tarantula moved onto it, she carried it over to its cage and gently set it down.

Which word can best replace the underlined word?
  A. fear
  B. calm
  C. pride

Name _____ **Date** _____

Jokes and Riddles

Andrew and Nicole got a joke book as a gift from their friend. They started reading different jokes and riddles to each other. Each time Andrew asked Nicole a riddle, Andrew would <u>verify</u> Nicole's answer. He did this by looking in the answer key to see if Nicole was right. Andrew didn't think Nicole would know the answer to "The more you have of it, the less you see," but she did. She knew the answer was "darkness."

Which word can best replace the underlined word?
A. write
B. check
C. copy

Dead End

Debbie and her mom were driving to a farm that was in the country. They were going to pick their own strawberries. They planned on making their own jam. After coming to a dead end, they knew they were lost. They turned around and asked the first person they saw for directions. The person told them to <u>proceed</u> in the same direction they were going and to turn left at the next intersection.

The underlined word means
A. continue.
B. turn around.
C. go back.

Name _____ **Date** _____

Free Diving

Free diving is when you descend under water without air tanks. People compete to see how far down they can dive in the water while using just one breath of air. First, they breathe in deeply, and their lungs <u>expand</u> to hold the air. As they descend and let out air, their lungs contract to the size of lemons. Free diving is not a sport for everyone.

Which words can best replace the underlined word?
- **A.** get smaller
- **B.** stay the same
- **C.** get bigger

Double Prints

Lauren took a beautiful picture of a bird. Michelle liked it so much that she asked Lauren if she could have a <u>duplicate</u> of the picture. Lauren said yes, so she made another print of the bird picture and gave it to Michelle.

The underlined word means
- **A.** frame.
- **B.** copy.
- **C.** cover.

Name _____ **Date** _____

Candy Calculations

Jonathon bought a small bag of candy to share with his friends. There were twenty pieces of candy in the bag. Jonathon evenly <u>distributed</u> the candy between himself and his four friends so that they could each have the same amount. They each got four pieces.

Which words can best replace the underlined word?
  A. collected together
  B. passed out
  C. gathered in

Good Friends

Jessie, Ken, Morgan, and Adam had such a good time skating in the park that they didn't want to go home. Instead, they <u>lingered</u>, talking and laughing among themselves. They enjoyed the moment and enjoyed spending time with the people they cared about.

Which word can best replace the underlined word?
  A. remained
  B. hurried
  C. created

Name _____ **Date** _____

Perfect Pies

Rose and her dad were going to make lots of apple pies. They needed different kinds of apples so they could see what kind makes the best-tasting pie. Rose and her dad wanted to enter some of their pies into a contest. Rose's dad wanted to know the <u>quantity</u> of apples needed. That way he could buy enough to make the pies and not have a lot left over.

The underlined word means

A. flavor.

B. color.

C. amount.

Whiz Kid

Javier is a very active five-year-old. He loves to climb and to play for hours at a time. He also has lots of special talents. Javier can read, write, and multiply! Older kids love to ask him multiplication questions because he gets them right every time. Everyone in the neighborhood thinks Javier is <u>brilliant</u>.

Which word can best replace the underlined word?

A. strong

B. smart

C. young

Name _____ **Date** _____

Leftover Dogs

After lunch, Ava helped put the leftover food away. She used a <u>transparent</u> bag that could be resealed and reused. She could see exactly how many hot dogs were inside the bag even after she sealed it.

The underlined word means
A. empty.
B. dark.
C. clear.

Late Fees

Records show that George Washington has two overdue library books. He checked out five books on October 5, 1789. He got them from the New York City Library. At that time, Washington was president, and New York was still the capital. If Washington were alive today and paid his late fees, he would have to pay more than $300,000! It's likely the library would not make him pay. Perhaps they would just ask for the books back. If he didn't pay for or return the books, they could <u>terminate</u> his library card. He would no longer be able to check out books.

Which word can best replace the underlined word?
A. cancel
B. purchase
C. continue

Name _____ Date _____

Complicated Conversions

Liam and Lily were going to build a doghouse. First, they looked at the directions. That's when they saw that the lengths were given in centimeters. Liam and Lily only had a yardstick that showed inches. To build the doghouse correctly, Liam and Lily had to first <u>convert</u> all the measurements from centimeters to inches.

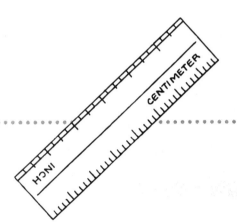

The underlined word means
  A. change.
  B. check.
  C. guess.

Unexpected Adventure

Dave and Daisy wanted to go on vacation. They decided to go to Ireland. There, they could rent a car and drive around the island. They could see castles, too. Dave and Daisy bought their tickets on the Internet. Finally, the day had arrived! They fell asleep as soon as they were seated on the plane. When they arrived at their destination, they were very confused. They were not in Ireland! They were in Iceland! They had made a simple typing <u>blunder</u> of just one letter, but it meant they were in the wrong country!

The underlined word means
  A. discovery.
  B. bargain.
  C. error.

Name _____ Date _____

Germ-Free

Which <u>two</u> statements are **facts**?

(A.) Washing hands with soap and warm water gets rid of most germs.
B. People should wash their hands twenty times a day.
(C.) Using hand sanitizer is an alternative for hand washing.

Learning Fractions

Which <u>two</u> statements are **opinions**?

A. A numerator is the top number in a fraction.
(B.) Adding fractions is easier than subtracting fractions.
(C.) Adding fractions is a good skill to learn.

Happy Fish

Which <u>two</u> statements are **facts**?

A. Fish like blue castles better than red treasure chests in aquariums.
(B.) Many freshwater fish or saltwater fish can be kept in aquariums.
(C.) Cleaning aquariums can help to maintain healthy fish.

Four-Legged Friends

Which <u>two</u> statements are **opinions**?

(A.) Big dog breeds like Dalmatians are better than smaller breeds like the Maltese.
B. The Dalmatian is a breed of dog first bred in the region of Dalmatia in the country of Croatia.
(C.) Dalmatians should be used as carriage dogs because that is what they were first bred for.

Beautiful Words

Which <u>two</u> statements are **facts**?

(A.) The cinquain is a style of poetry in which the lines do not need to rhyme.
(B.) Limericks, haikus, and acrostics are different types of poetry.
C. Poems sound better when they rhyme.

Venomous Kings

Which <u>two</u> statements are **opinions**?

(A.) King cobras are the best parents in the animal kingdom because the female makes a nest for her eggs and then stays in the nest until the eggs hatch.
(B.) Everyone should want a king cobra in their garden, as they can help to keep other snakes away.
C. The king cobra is the world's longest venomous snake, and it preys mostly on other snakes.

Name _____ Date _____

Math Minute

Which <u>two</u> statements are **facts**?

A. Adding 2 + 2 + 2 + 2 is the same as multiplying 2 × 4.
B. Learning basic multiplication is an easy thing to do.
C. One sign for multiplication is the × symbol.

Moon-Walking

Which <u>two</u> statements are **opinions**?

A. Neil Armstrong was the first person to set foot on the moon.
B. Landing on the moon was the greatest human achievement.
C. Rather than sending another space probe or rover, an astronaut should be sent to Mars.

A Lot of Feet

Which <u>two</u> statements are **facts**?

A. One mile is longer than one kilometer.
B. One mile is equal to 5,280 feet.
C. Running one mile is fairly easy to do.

Beautiful Brides

Which <u>two</u> statements are **opinions**?

A. The most beautiful wedding dresses are the ones with long trains.
B. Most brides wear white wedding dresses.
C. Weddings are more fun to attend when people dance.

Fifty Nifty States

Which <u>two</u> statements are **facts**?

A. There are 50 states in the United States of America.
B. Alaska and Hawaii are not connected to the 48 contiguous states.
C. California and New York are the best states to live in.

Dangerous Dinner

Which <u>two</u> statements are **opinions**?

A. The very poisonous pufferfish is eaten on purpose by some people.
B. People should never eat pufferfish, even when it is prepared by specially-trained chefs.
C. Restaurants should not be allowed to have pufferfish on their menus.

Name _____ **Date** _____

Honest Abe

OK!

Which <u>two</u> statements are **facts**?

   A. Abraham Lincoln was the greatest leader in U.S. history.

   B. Lincoln never slept in the current Lincoln Bedroom in the White House, but he did use the room as his office.

   C. President Abraham Lincoln's picture appears on the five-dollar bill.

Digital Mail

Which <u>two</u> statements are **opinions**?

   A. Email is the easiest way of communicating with people long-distance.

   B. Some people can send emails from their cell phones.

   C. Emailing people is better than talking to people.

Seven Wonders

Which <u>two</u> statements are **facts**?

   A. The Great Pyramid of Giza is the only one of the Seven Wonders of the Ancient World that is still standing.

   B. Four of the Seven Wonders of the Ancient World were destroyed by earthquakes.

   C. The greatest wonder of the Seven Wonders of the Ancient World was the Lighthouse of Alexandria because it was the only one that helped to save lives.

Colorful Opinions

Which <u>two</u> statements are **opinions**?

   A. Dark colors are too dull to use in paintings.

   B. Some colors can be mixed to make new colors.

   C. Colors look their best when not mixed with too many other colors.

Reduce and Reuse

Which <u>two</u> statements are **facts**?

   A. Washing and reusing dishes is always better than using paper plates.

   B. Plastic plates can be recycled and made into something new.

   C. Many cities have recycling programs that pick up recyclables from people's homes.

Four Great Inventions

Which <u>two</u> statements are **opinions**?

   A. China is most famous for what is known as the Four Great Inventions.

   B. The compass, paper making, and printing are three of China's Four Great Inventions.

   C. The bristle toothbrush should be on the list of the Four Great Inventions instead of gunpowder.

Name _____ Date _____

$10 - 5 = \cancel{X} \\ 5$

Making Money

Which <u>two</u> statements are **facts**?

A. Some countries, like Canada, no longer mint pennies.

B. In 2011, a gold coin was minted in Australia that was worth more than 50 million dollars.

C. Countries should only mint coins that are worth at least five cents.

Wonderful Words

Which <u>two</u> statements are **opinions**?

A. Words in a dictionary are listed in alphabetical order.

B. Students should not spend time in school learning how to use a dictionary when they could be doing math.

C. Dictionary definitions are sometimes hard to understand.

Different Angles

Which <u>two</u> statements are **facts**?

A. An angle less than 90 degrees is called an acute angle.

B. Acute angles are the easiest angles to measure.

C. Obtuse angles are those larger than 90 degrees.

Four-Sided Fun

Which <u>two</u> statements are **opinions**?

A. It is fun to form patterns with different shapes.

B. A rectangle is an easier quadrilateral to draw than a square.

C. All quadrilaterals have four sides.

Math's Best Friend

Which <u>two</u> statements are **facts**?

A. Calculators can solve math problems very quickly.

B. Calculators can solve basic or complex math problems.

C. It is not fair to use a calculator on a math test.

The Dead Sea

Which <u>two</u> statements are **opinions**?

A. The Dead Sea is a lake in Israel that is so salty that you can't sink in it.

B. People should not be allowed to splash water in the Dead Sea because the high salt content of the water can really hurt your eyes.

C. Swimming in the Dead Sea is something that everyone should do at least once in his or her lifetime.

Name _____ Date _____

A Full Deck

Which <u>two</u> statements are **facts**?

A. A full deck of playing cards has 52 cards.
B. Playing card games is a great way to enjoy time with friends.
C. "Go Fish" is a card game usually played by two or more players.

Juice It Up

Which <u>two</u> statements are **opinions**?

A. The best juices are apple, orange, and pineapple juice.
B. Milk, juice, and water should be the only drinks sold in schools.
C. Juicers are machines that squeeze juice from fruits or vegetables.

Changing Directions

Which <u>two</u> statements are **facts**?

A. English is an easy language to read because it is read from left to right.
B. Arabic is read from right to left.
C. Traditional Japanese is written top to bottom and read from right to left.

Old Glory

Which <u>two</u> statements are **opinions**?

A. The United States flag is red, white, and blue.
B. The United States flag has the nicest colors.
C. "Old Glory" is the best nickname for the United States flag.

Meet the Swiftlets

Which <u>two</u> statements are **facts**?

A. The nests of cave swiftlets are made into a soup that is considered to be a real delicacy.
B. A cave swiftlet's nest is made mostly out of its saliva.
C. Cave swiftlet nests should not be harvested even if they are valuable.

Island Life

Which <u>two</u> statements are **opinions**?

A. Although Australia is a continent, it should still be called an island.
B. Greenland is the largest island in the world.
C. If Australia is called an island, then Antarctica should be called one, too.

Name _____ Date _____

Spooky Sounds

Stephanie woke up thirsty in the middle of the night. She wanted to get a drink of water from the kitchen. When she sat up, she heard a spooky sound coming from the living room. <u>Stephanie decided to go back to sleep instead.</u>

The underlined statement is the **effect**. What is the **cause**?

A. She heard a spooky sound.
B. She wasn't thirsty anymore.
C. She was too tired to get up.

Come Back, Ollie

Mason was walking his dog Ollie along the trail. <u>Suddenly, Ollie spotted a cat.</u> Ollie took off running after the cat. The leash flew out of Mason's hand! Mason spent the next twenty minutes chasing after his dog.

The underlined statement is the **cause**. What is the **effect**?

A. Ollie's leash ripped.
B. Ollie ignored the cat.
C. Ollie ran after the cat.

Wrap Star

Melanie was wrapping a birthday present using colorful wrapping paper. The present came in a large box. She laid the wrapping paper over the present. Part of the box was still showing. <u>The wrapping paper wasn't big enough to wrap the entire box.</u>

The underlined statement is the **effect**. What is the **cause**?

A. The present came in a big box.
B. The wrapping paper was colorful.
C. Melanie wanted to use a gift bag.

Name _____ **Date** _____

Facing His Fears

At the October Fair, Ethan dared Justin to go into the haunted house. Justin was nervous, but <u>he wanted to seem brave</u>. Justin walked in and followed the path through the entire haunted house. It really wasn't as scary as he had thought. In fact, he thought of ways he could make it scarier for next year.

The underlined statement is the **cause**. What is the **effect**?

   A. Justin was too nervous to go in.
   B. Justin walked into the haunted house.
   C. Justin dared Ethan to go with him.

Time for Tea

Mom wanted to drink some tea. She put water in the tea kettle, put it on the stove, and turned on the burner. After a few minutes, <u>the tea kettle began whistling loudly</u>, meaning that the water inside was boiling. Mom turned off the burner that was under the kettle. Now, Mom could enjoy her favorite tea.

The underlined statement is the **effect**. What is the **cause**?

   A. Mom put the water into a tea kettle.
   B. Mom used a kettle to heat up water.
   C. Mom wanted to enjoy some tea.

Living in Slow Motion

Sloths are mammals that seem to live life in slow motion. They can spend half of their lives sleeping. <u>They eat mostly leaves</u>, so they don't get much energy from their food. Sloths conserve energy by doing everything slowly. Even their digestion is slow. When a sloth eats some leaves, it may take one month for the food to move from its stomach to its small intestines!

The underlined statement is the **cause**. What is the **effect**?

   A. Sloths have a much slower digestion system than people.
   B. Sloths eat in slow motion.
   C. Sloths don't get much energy from their food.

Name _____ **Date** _____

Favorite Photo

After taking pictures at her little brother's birthday party, Kendra was picking out her favorite ones. Kendra found one photo of her brother that she really liked; he was blowing out the candles that were on his cake. Kendra wanted to share the picture with her friends. <u>Kendra emailed the picture to everyone</u> so that they could see it.

The underlined statement is the **effect**. What is the **cause**?

   A. Kendra wanted to share the picture.
   B. Kendra liked taking pictures.
   C. Kendra's brother blew out the candles.

Hidden Treasure

While playing at the park, James and Leona found a shoebox hidden in the bushes. They opened up the shoebox and found that it was full of money. <u>James and Leona turned in the money to the police station</u>. The police gave James and Leona a reward.

The underlined statement is the **cause**. What is the **effect**?

   A. James and Leona found a shoebox at the park.
   B. The police gave James and Leona a reward.
   C. The shoebox was full of money.

Bake Sale

Amber and Ari volunteered to make cupcakes for the school bake sale. On Friday morning, they mixed enough batter for seven dozen cupcakes. Amber and Ari spent the day baking and frosting. At the bake sale, the cupcakes were sold for fifty cents each. <u>The school earned $42.00 from cupcake sales</u>.

The underlined statement is the **effect**. What is the **cause**?

   A. The volunteers didn't make enough cupcakes.
   B. The cupcakes were sold for fifty cents each.
   C. The cupcakes were free for students.

Name _____ **Date** _____

New Flavor

The bakery gave away one free cookie to every customer. The owner had a new flavor that he wanted to promote. At first, people didn't think it would taste good. <u>After tasting it, people changed their minds</u>. They bought more cookies of the new flavor than any other cookie in the bakery.

The underlined statement is the **cause**. What is the **effect**?

   A. People said that they didn't want to taste the new cookie.
   B. The bakery gave away one free cookie to every customer.
   C. People bought more cookies of the new flavor than any other cookie in the bakery.

Too Hot!

Yesterday, the track team practiced in 90-degree weather. Derrick ran one mile as a warm-up and then trained with his coach for about an hour. <u>By the end of practice, Derrick was wishing he had joined the swim team</u>! Derrick thought swimming in the hot weather would be more fun.

The underlined statement is the **effect**. What is the **cause**?

   A. Derrick didn't like the track team and wanted to switch sports.
   B. Derrick's feet were sore from running a one-mile warm up and then practicing for an hour with the coach.
   C. Derrick would have preferred swimming in hot weather.

Riddle Restlessness

Sam couldn't get to sleep because he couldn't stop thinking about a riddle Juan had asked him to solve. Juan said, "What word becomes shorter when you add two letters to it?" <u>Sam finally thought of the answer to Juan's question</u>. "If you add the two letters 'e' and 'r' to *short*, you get *shorter*," he thought. Smiling, Sam turned over and went right to sleep.

The underlined statement is the **cause**. What is the **effect**?

   A. Sam was able to fall asleep.
   B. Sam couldn't get to sleep.
   C. Juan had asked Sam to solve a riddle.

Name _____ **Date** _____

No Movie Tonight

Everyone in the movie theater was wondering what was going on. The movie was skipping every few seconds. <u>The theater manager stopped the movie and turned on the lights</u>. He gave coupons to everyone. The coupons made it so everyone could go back and watch the movie for free once it was working correctly.

The underlined statement is the **effect**. What is the **cause**?

A. The movie was skipping.

B. The theater manager passed out coupons to everybody.

C. Everyone wanted to come back to watch the movie again.

Late-Night Snack

Katya didn't usually eat snacks after dinner. One evening, <u>she ate a snack right before bed</u>. When Katya went to bed that night, she had trouble falling asleep. After she tossed and turned for an hour, Katya decided that having snacks before bed was not a good idea.

The underlined statement is the **cause**. What is the **effect**?

A. Katya had another snack.

B. Katya had trouble falling asleep.

C. Katya was hungry.

The Trouble with Texting

Every month, Rodney is allowed to send up to 250 text messages. If he sends more than that, there will be a charge for each additional text. Last month, he sent 277 text messages. <u>Rodney's mom made him use his allowance to pay for the extra texts</u>. Rodney wants his mom to purchase a different texting plan.

The underlined statement is the **effect**. What is the **cause**?

A. Rodney is going to start paying for unlimited texts.

B. Rodney is not allowed to send text messages.

C. Rodney sent too many text messages.

Name _____ **Date** _____

Vote for Dane

Dane was running for fifth-grade president. <u>He gave a convincing speech about why people should vote for him</u>. Dane's classmates liked his speech. On Election Day, Dane was elected to be fifth-grade president.

The underlined statement is the **cause**. What is the **effect**?

  A. Dane's classmates talked a lot about his speech.
  B. Dane's classmates elected him to be fifth-grade president.
  C. Dane decided to run for fifth-grade president.

Lock It Up

Make sure you lock up your bike every time you ride it somewhere. Julianne forgot to lock up her bike when she rode it to the park for soccer practice. When practice was over, she realized that <u>her bike had been stolen</u>.

The underlined statement is the **effect**. What is the **cause**?

  A. Soccer practice was in the park.
  B. Someone broke Julianne's bike lock.
  C. Julianne forgot to lock up her bike.

Google It

Google is an Internet search engine. Every year, searches on Google for the word "fitness" increase in January. Then, in the following months, the number of searches decreases dramatically. Everyone knows why. <u>It is because a common New Year's resolution is to get in shape</u>.

The underlined statement is the **cause**. What is the **effect**?

  A. The number of people searching the word "fitness" goes up in January.
  B. Everyone knows that people make New Year's resolutions.
  C. People use Google's search engine more in January than any other month.

Name _____ **Date** _____

Grandfather's Chest

<u>The wooden chest had to be cut open with a saw</u>. The chest belongs to Grandfather Smith. He had valuables locked inside, and he lost his only key. Inside, there was a picture of Grandmother Smith, Grandfather Smith's collection of baseball cards, and a small box of jewels.

The underlined statement is the **effect**. What is the **cause**?

A. The only key to unlock the chest was lost.
B. Grandfather Smith lost his baseball cards.
C. The wood was going to be used as firewood.

Protecting the Planet

Blair saves plastic bottles and aluminum cans. <u>She takes the bottles and cans to the recycling center</u>. She gets money for recycling them. Blair is happy knowing that the old plastic and aluminum will be turned into something new.

The underlined statement is the **cause**. What is the **effect**?

A. Blair pays money for bottles and cans.
B. The bottles and cans are turned into something new.
C. Blair saves her plastic bottles and aluminum cans.

Chili Cook-Off

Eleven people were ready to compete in the chili cook-off. They would each have to try to prepare the best-tasting chili. The judges would taste the chili. Then they would decide who the winner was. Everyone got their ingredients ready. The head judge said, "You may begin!" <u>All the contestants immediately began cooking</u>.

The underlined statement is the **effect**.   What is the **cause**?

A. The judges were ready to taste the chili.
B. The winning contestant had the best-tasting chili.
C. The chili cook-off started.

Name _____ **Date** _____

A Peek Under the Sea

<u>Kevin visited the Sea Life Aquarium.</u> He saw hundreds of different fish, some sea turtles, and several other ocean creatures. He even got to hold a sea star. Kevin thought the trip to the aquarium was a lot of fun.

The underlined statement is the **cause**. What is the **effect**?

A. Kevin only saw fish at the aquarium.
B. Kevin got to see lots of ocean creatures.
C. Kevin did not like the trip to the aquarium.

Library Day

Every Thursday is library day for Jay and Isabella's class. On Wednesdays, the teacher always reminds the students to bring in their library books for the following day. Both Jay and Isabella forgot their library books at home. <u>They were not allowed to check out any new books.</u> They had to bring the other books back first.

The underlined statement is the **effect**. What is the **cause**?

A. Jay and Isabella forgot to return their library books.
B. Jay and Isabella did not hear the teacher's reminder.
C. On Wednesday, Jay and Isabella checked out books.

Protecting the Paws

The Iditarod is a great dog-sledding race that takes place in Alaska. One of the rules is that <u>dog mushers must carry a certain number of booties for each dog.</u> Dogs' feet don't easily get frostbitten, so why the booties? The booties are needed to protect the dog's feet from being scraped up or cut on the ice.

The underlined statement is the **cause**. What is the **effect**?

A. The dogs' feet get frostbitten easily.
B. The dogs sometimes get ice balls between their toes.
C. The dogs' feet are protected from the ice.

Name _____ **Date** _____

Filling the Buckets

Last weekend, Addie's grandparents took her blueberry picking. She and her grandparents were each given small buckets when they arrived at the field. <u>Addie filled her bucket to the top with blueberries.</u> She shared the fresh blueberries with her brother and sister that evening.

The underlined statement is the **effect**. What is the **cause**?

- **A.** Addie was grocery shopping.
- **B.** Addie shared her blueberries.
- **C.** Addie went blueberry picking.

Camera-Shy

My cousin <u>Linda did not want her picture taken</u> the day of the family reunion. She hid her face every time she saw the camera. It became a game to see who could get a picture of Linda's face.

The underlined statement is the **cause**. What is the **effect**?

- **A.** Linda attended the family reunion.
- **B.** Linda hid her face when she saw the camera.
- **C.** Linda wanted to be a part of a picture game.

Adoption Day

"Can we get a kitten?" Alex asked his parents. After discussing the responsibilities of having a kitten, Alex's parents said they could adopt one. <u>Alex and his parents went to the animal shelter to see the kittens.</u> One kitten went right up to Alex and began to purr at his feet. "This is the one!" said Alex.

The underlined statement is the **effect**. What is the **cause**?

- **A.** Alex's parents said they could adopt a kitten.
- **B.** Alex and his parents went looking for their lost kitten.
- **C.** Alex chose the kitten that purred at his feet.

Name _____ **Date** _____

Rained Out

On Friday, Maggie went online in order to check the weather forecast for the next day. The weather website showed that, on Saturday, <u>there was a 100% chance of rain in her city</u>. Maggie decided that she would skip her morning walk that day.

The underlined statement is the **cause**. What is the **effect**?

   A. Maggie went online in order to check the weekend weather forecast.
   B. Maggie decided to go for a morning walk.
   C. Maggie decided that she would skip her morning walk.

Celebrating Safely

July 4th is Independence Day. Some people celebrate by lighting fireworks in their neighborhoods. <u>In many cities, though, it is against the law for people to light fireworks</u>. This is because fireworks can be dangerous. The cities don't want to risk the chance of fires or of people getting hurt.

The underlined statement is the **effect**. What is the **cause**?

   A. Fireworks can be dangerous.
   B. People can see a fireworks show.
   C. Some neighborhoods are very crowded.

Talking Eggs

A mother crocodile or alligator lays all of her eggs at the same time. This group of eggs is called a *clutch*. These eggs often "talk" to each other. <u>The hatchlings inside the eggs tap from inside their shells</u>. They are communicating with the other eggs in their clutch. Scientists think this tapping helps the hatchlings to hatch all at the same time.

The underlined statement is the **cause**. What is the **effect**?

   A. The mother crocodile or alligator lays a clutch of eggs.
   B. The eggs in a clutch all hatch about the same time.
   C. The hatchlings are communicating with their mother.

Getting Ready for Bed

1. Elijah started his bedtime routine at 8:00 last night.

2. Right before he went to sleep, Elijah read a story with his mom.

3. Next, he put on a clean pair of pajamas from his drawer.

4. He started by taking a shower and brushing his teeth.

What is the correct sequence?

   A. 1, 3, 4, 2
   B. 1, 2, 3, 4
   C. 1, 4, 3, 2

Wooden Airplane

1. Eric received a wooden airplane kit as a gift for his birthday.

2. Once completed, Eric played with his airplane toy a little bit every day.

3. Eric painted the body of the plane red and the wings blue.

4. When the paint dried, Eric added some stickers to give the airplane a nice design.

Which sentence comes first?

   A. Sentence 1
   B. Sentence 2
   C. Sentence 3

Name _____ **Date** _____

Almost There

1. To buy the new book she wants, Tonya needs to save $1.46 more.

2. Tonya was happy to know she had saved $13.54 in her piggy bank.

3. Tonya emptied her piggy bank so she could add up how much money was in it.

4. Tonya counted all the money that was in her piggy bank.

What is the correct sequence?

A. 1, 2, 4, 3
B. 3, 4, 2, 1
C. 3, 1, 4, 2

Crossword Support

1. Harper started with the "down" words first because she thought the clues were easy.

2. Harper started on a science crossword puzzle for homework.

3. Harper's sister helped explain what the clues meant, and Harper finished the rest of the puzzle on her own.

4. Harper asked her sister for help with the "across" words because she didn't understand the clues.

Which sentence comes third?

A. Sentence 1
B. Sentence 2
C. Sentence 4

Name _____ **Date** _____

Rainy-Day Schedule

1. It was raining so hard at school today that no one was allowed to play outside during lunch.

2. We all had to eat lunch and play quietly inside the classroom instead.

3. At one point, board games and coloring books were lying all around the classroom.

4. When lunch was almost over, the teacher told us to clean up.

What is the correct sequence?
   A. 1, 4, 3, 2
   B. 2, 1, 3, 4
   C. 1, 2, 3, 4

Heading East

1. The Ozark Mountains in Arkansas were Owen and Anna's favorite stop on their trip.

2. Owen and Anna stopped for lunch in Santa Fe, the capital of New Mexico.

3. Owen and Anna left Arizona early in the morning for their road trip east across the United States.

4. When they crossed the border into Oklahoma, Owen said, "Texas is the second-largest state, and now we're through it!"

What sentences comes last?
   A. Sentence 1
   B. Sentence 2
   C. Sentence 4

Name _____ **Date** _____

Pumpkin Makeover

1. Using a black marker, Ted drew silly faces on the pumpkins.

2. Ted lit candles that were inside the newly carved pumpkins.

3. Ted went to the pumpkin patch and picked out two pumpkins.

4. On Halloween morning, Ted carved the pumpkins along the black lines.

What is the correct sequence?

A. 4, 1, 3, 2

B. 3, 1, 4, 2

C. 3, 4, 2, 1

Animal Reports

1. Ms. Toms told her students that they would need to write a report about their favorite animal.

2. They used their books to learn more about their animals in order to write their reports.

3. Zoey chose to write her report about pandas, and Steven chose to write about rattlesnakes.

4. Steve and Zoey both went to the library and checked out six books each about his and her animal.

Which sentence comes first?

A. Sentence 1

B. Sentence 3

C. Sentence 4

Name _____ **Date** _____

Yard Work

1. Right after mowing, Brooklyn emptied the clippings into the compost pile.

2. Brooklyn took the lawnmower out of the shed.

3. Brooklyn filled the mower with gas and mowed the grass in her front yard.

4. Then, Brooklyn swept up the walkways, finishing the job.

What is the correct sequence?

  A. 2, 1, 4, 3

  B. 2, 3, 1, 4

  C. 2, 4, 1, 3

Not the Same

1. Yori showed his older brother the list of words that he wrote.

2. Yori thought of *hair* and *hare*, *be* and *bee*, *our* and *hour*, and *ate* and *eight*.

3. His brother noticed that Yori had written sets of homophones.

4. For homework, Yori's teacher asked the class to list pairs of words that sound the same but have different spellings and meanings.

Which sentence comes second?

  A. Sentence 2

  B. Sentence 4

  C. Sentence 3

Name _____ Date _____

Hostage Negotiators

1. A large, male sea otter won't release the pup until the mother sea otter pays a ransom.

2. When the mother sea otter pops up to the surface with a squid, she finds that her pup has been taken hostage!

3. The mother otter quickly gives the squid to the male otter, and now that the ransom has been paid, the male otter releases the pup.

4. A mother sea otter wraps her pup in kelp so that it won't float away as she dives for food.

What is the correct sequence?
  A. 3, 4, 1, 2
  B. 2, 4, 3, 1
  C. 4, 2, 1, 3

The Quiet Prince

1. Piper turned on her computer and typed her story.

2. Piper printed out the story on white paper and added a drawing of the prince to the back.

3. Mrs. Crane told Piper's class that they had to turn in a typed story and include at least one drawing.

4. In her notebook, Piper wrote a story about a prince who wouldn't speak.

Which sentence comes third?
  A. Sentence 2
  B. Sentence 4
  C. Sentence 1

Name _____ **Date** _____

Dirty Dishes

1. Hunter and Lucy unloaded the clean dishes that were already in the dishwasher.

2. After dinner, Hunter and Lucy offered to wash the dishes.

3. Once the dishwasher was full of dirty dishes, Hunter and Lucy put in the soap and started it.

4. Hunter and Lucy rinsed the dishes from the sink and placed them in the dishwasher.

What is the correct sequence?

  A. 2, 1, 4, 3

  B. 1, 3, 2, 4

  C. 3, 4, 2, 1

Puzzled

1. Don bought a new 1,000-piece puzzle to put together.

2. Don had a hard time working on his puzzle by himself because many of the pieces were the same color.

3. They liked the finished puzzle so much that they chose to frame and hang it in their room.

4. Don's older brother helped him with the puzzle.

Which sentence comes last?

  A. Sentence 4

  B. Sentence 3

  C. Sentence 1

Name _____ **Date** _____

A Busy Day

1. She spent the first few hours of her day in the back yard trying to chase birds.

2. By the afternoon, Chance was so hungry that she ate two bowls of food and drank an entire bowl of water.

3. Chance, our very energetic dog, went outside as soon as the sun came out this morning.

4. Chance rested all evening because she'd had such a busy day.

What is the correct sequence?
- **A.** 2, 4, 1, 3
- **B.** 3, 1, 2, 4
- **C.** 3, 4, 2, 1

Clean Floor

1. The lights in the movie theater were turned down, and the previews started showing on the big screen.

2. After the movie ended, I looked around and saw that I had not spilled any popcorn onto the ground.

3. It got so dark in the theater that I could barely see my popcorn!

4. Pretty soon, my eyes were used to the dark.

Which sentence comes third?
- **A.** Sentence 1
- **B.** Sentence 2
- **C.** Sentence 4

Name _____ **Date** _____

Costume Party

1. Sarah was surprised when some friends arrived wearing regular clothes.

2. Sarah invited her friends over to her house for a costume party.

3. Everyone stood together for a group picture at the end of the night.

4. Sarah framed the picture so that she'd always remember her fun party.

What is the correct sequence?
  A. 2, 1, 3, 4
  B. 2, 3, 4, 1
  C. 1, 2, 3, 4

Book Report

1. Kurt pressed the button on his computer to turn it on.

2. Using the computer, Kurt started typing his book report.

3. Every few minutes, Kurt pressed the save button so he would not lose the words he had already typed.

4. When Kurt was done typing, he read through his book report in order to fix any typing mistakes.

Which sentence comes second?
  A. Sentence 1
  B. Sentence 2
  C. Sentence 3

74

Name _____ **Date** _____

Water Rising

1. Then he paused to think.

2. Ruby said, "You are on a boat. On the side of the boat is a ladder that has six steps. Each step is one foot apart from the next. It starts to rain, and the water level rises six feet. How many steps on the ladder are underwater?"

3. Daniel was about to say that all the steps were under the water.

4. "None!" Daniel said. "All the steps stay above water because the boat rises with the water."

What is the correct sequence?
- **A.** 2, 4, 3, 1
- **B.** 2, 1, 3, 4
- **C.** 2, 3, 1, 4

Falling like Dominoes

1. The first domino fell, tipping over the ones behind it.

2. Logan lined up a long row of dominoes across the tile floor.

3. The entire row of dominoes was tipped over within five seconds.

4. Gently, Logan tapped on the first domino in the row.

Which sentence comes third?
- **A.** Sentence 1
- **B.** Sentence 2
- **C.** Sentence 3

Name _____ Date _____

Where's Mom?

1. Jade's mom dropped Jade off at her grandma's house and said she'd be back in 180 minutes.

2. Jade's grandma said that 180 minutes is the same as three hours, so her mom wasn't coming back for two more hours.

3. Jade had thought that if someone said the time in minutes, it was always less than an hour, but now she knew differently.

4. One hour later, Jade asked why her mom was late getting back.

What is the correct sequence?
   A. 3, 4, 2, 1
   B. 2, 4, 3, 1
   C. 1, 4, 2, 3

Path to Success

1. When Colin's aunt saw his report card, she told Colin she was proud of him.

2. They went out to dinner to celebrate.

3. Colin opened his report card and saw that five out of six grades were very good.

4. When they were leaving the restaurant, Colin told his aunt he would continue to work hard and keep up his grades.

Which sentence comes third?
   A. Sentence 1
   B. Sentence 2
   C. Sentence 3

Name _____ **Date** _____

Beautiful Morning

1. Victor said to Laila, "Now we can see the sun rise in the continental United States before anyone else."

2. Laila said, "I thought the sunrise was beautiful."

3. They used flashlights to make their way up to the top of Cadillac Mountain in Acadia, Maine.

4. Victor and Laila got up while it was still dark.

What is the correct sequence?
   A. 4, 3, 1, 2
   B. 4, 1, 2, 3
   C. 3, 1, 4, 2

Top Five

1. Miguel wrote Brazil down at the bottom of his list.

2. Miguel was listing in order (from biggest to smallest) the five largest countries in the world, so he put Russia on the top of his list.

3. China was next on Miguel's list, followed by the United States.

4. Miguel put Canada as the second-largest country, even though Antarctica has a bigger land mass.

Which sentence comes third?
   A. Sentence 2
   B. Sentence 3
   C. Sentence 4

Black and White

1. The female makes a long trek back to the sea so that she can eat.

2. The male and female Emperor penguins trek over the ice for 30 to 70 miles to get to a breeding colony.

3. When the female returns, she picks her mate out of the thousands of other penguins by his call.

4. The female lays a single egg and carefully transfers it over to her mate, who balances it on the top of his feet and keeps it in his brood patch.

What is the correct sequence?
  A. 1, 2, 3, 4
  B. 2, 4, 1, 3
  C. 3, 1, 4, 2

Dressing in Layers

1. Jessica wore a tank top and a T-shirt with a warm sweatshirt over them.

2. As the day got warmer, Jessica took off her sweatshirt.

3. It was cold in the morning, so Jessica picked out three different tops to wear in layers along with her jeans.

4. By the afternoon, Jessica was only wearing her jeans and a tank top.

Which sentence comes second?
  A. Sentence 1
  B. Sentence 3
  C. Sentence 2

78

Name _____ **Date** _____

Frozen Bubbles

1. The small bubbles froze in the air and then shattered on the ground!

2. Halley and Oscar put on their snow pants and went outside with their bubble mixture.

3. They mixed one-half cup of dishwashing liquid, two cups of water, and a drop of food coloring.

4. One cold winter morning, Halley and Oscar wondered what would happen if they blew bubbles outside.

What is the correct sequence?
  A. 4, 1, 3, 2
  B. 4, 2, 1, 3
  C. 4, 3, 2, 1

Visiting Mom

1. After her plane landed in New York, Fatima took a taxi to her mom's house.

2. Fatima bought a ticket to fly to New York to see her mom over Mother's Day weekend.

3. She packed a small bag of clothes because her trip was only a few days long.

4. Fatima's mom was sad to see her daughter leave.

Which sentence comes last?
  A. Sentence 4
  B. Sentence 2
  C. Sentence 3

Name _____ Date _____

Metamorphosis

1. After a month, Leif and Melody wondered when the chrysalises would hatch.

2. Leif and Melody put two caterpillars and some leaves in a cage.

3. Leif and Melody took pictures of their butterflies before letting them go.

4. One day, they didn't see the caterpillars anymore.

What is the correct sequence?
   A. 1, 3, 4, 2
   B. 2, 4, 1, 3
   C. 3, 2, 1, 4

Masked Men

1. Tanner said, "Oh no! I hope nothing bad happened to him."

2. Bradley said, "My friend left home. He made three left turns, and then he found two masked men waiting for him."

3. Tanner said, "And the other masked man must have been the catcher!"

4. Bradley said, "There was nothing to worry about. One of the men was the umpire."

Which sentence comes last?
   A. Sentence 1
   B. Sentence 2
   C. Sentence 3

80

Name _____ **Date** _____

Be My Valentine

Today was a fun day at school because all the students were allowed to exchange valentines. In art class the day before, the students decorated shoeboxes. They pasted red and white hearts on them. When the students exchanged their valentines, they put them in each other's boxes. While the students opened their boxes, they ate special heart-shaped cookies. Then the teacher told them a story about taking care of each other and giving.

Most likely, **when** did this happen?

  A. on February 14
  B. on March 17
  C. on October 31

A Special Day

Lots of people were holding cameras. They were waiting to see their loved ones. Soon, music played, and a line of people came in wearing special caps on their heads and long gowns. After they sat down, a man talked about how well they all had done and said that he would miss them. He called everyone's name and gave them each an award called a diploma.

Most likely, **where** is everyone?

  A. at a wedding
  B. at a graduation
  C. at a concert

Name _____ **Date** _____

Schedule Change

Pat used to exercise every night, but it made her have trouble sleeping. Pat found that she had lots of energy after exercising, so she changed her exercise time. Now, when Pat goes to work she has lots of energy. She doesn't feel tired all day, and she no longer has trouble going to sleep.

Most likely, **when** does Pat exercise?

   A. early in the morning

   B. in the middle of the day

   C. late at night

Spoiling the Grandkids

"There were lions that jumped through big hoops! People were riding elephants, and funny guys with red noses did some amazing tricks!" Tyler and Sally told their parents when they came home. "And to think that it was all inside one big tent!" they added. Tyler and Sally's parents could tell that Tyler and Sally had enjoyed their time with their grandparents.

Most likely, **where** did Tyler and Sally go with their grandparents?

   A. camping

   B. to the zoo

   C. to a circus

Name _____   Date _____

Tough Run

Paige is training for a 100-mile endurance run. Paige will have 30 hours to complete her run. There will be aid stations on the way where Paige can get food and water. Some endurance runs are in the mountains, but Paige is going to run in a desert. To train, Paige will try to run when the sun is out. She knows that, when running, it is important to drink lots of water. She always carries a bottle of water with her, and if she needs to, she can stop and refill it. After Paige finishes her training runs, she often goes for a swim in her backyard pool. At the end of Paige's runs, her shirt is usually soaked.

Most likely, **how** does Paige's shirt get wet?
- **A.** She spills her water bottle.
- **B.** She sweats.
- **C.** She swims with her shirt on.

Machu Picchu

Trent was going to see the ancient city of Machu Picchu. After flying to Peru, he would hike high in the mountains. He would go 7,970 feet above sea level. Machu Picchu was built by the Incas around 1450. It was abandoned a century later. The city was locally known, but outsiders didn't know about it until 1911. The city's buildings were built out of stone. It is still a mystery how some of the biggest stones were moved. The wheel wasn't used. It may be that hundreds of people pushed each stone up inclined planes. An inclined plane is a flat surface tilted at an angle.

Most likely, Machu Picchu is in **what** mountain range?
- **A.** the Rockies
- **B.** the Appalachians
- **C.** the Andes

Name _____ Date _____

Busy Schedule

On Tuesdays, Eve has dance class after school. On Wednesdays, she takes a Spanish class. She goes straight to softball practice after that. Every Thursday, she takes piano lessons. Eve often gets her schedule confused because she's involved in so many programs. Eve sprained her ankle on Monday and has to use crutches to walk around.

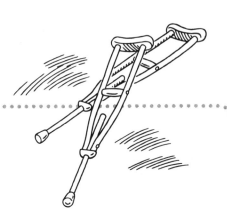

Most likely, **what** will Eve do this week?
   A. go to Spanish class and her piano lesson
   B. go to dance class and Spanish class
   C. go to her piano lesson and softball practice

Heading to Luckyville

Brandon and Sasha packed their suitcases with enough clothes for five days. They went to the station with their tickets to Luckyville. Aunt Wanda would pick them up when they got there. Brandon and Sasha made several stops along the way to Luckyville. They even had to make an emergency stop because something was on the tracks. When they got off, Brandon and Sasha saw Aunt Wanda waiting for them.

Most likely, **how** did Brandon and Sasha travel?
   A. by bus
   B. by plane
   C. by train

Name _____ **Date** _____

Out of Focus

Austin wears eyeglasses to school every day. Without them, he has trouble seeing things that are far away, like the clock and the whiteboard. One Saturday, Austin went to a pool party with his friends. Austin's friends were surprised to see him without his glasses. Everyone had fun diving for coins at the bottom of the pool. When it was Austin's turn, he found the coins by touch. He didn't even need to open his eyes.

Most likely, **how** was Austin able to play without his glasses?
- **A.** His eyesight got better overnight.
- **B.** He took medicine that made his eyesight better.
- **C.** At the party, he didn't need to see things that were far away.

Recess Time

The students in Ms. Stamper's class sat in differently-colored table groups to work on their art projects. Ms. Stamper asked everyone to get ready to go outside for recess. The students hurried to pick up their scraps and to clean any glue off the tabletops. Ms. Stamper looked around the room. She said that the orange group could go out to recess first.

Most likely, **why** did the orange group get to go to recess first?
- **A.** They were the first group to have a clean table.
- **B.** They were the first group to glue their scraps together.
- **C.** They were the first group to finish their art projects.

Name _____ Date _____

Office Visit

Melissa sees many patients each day at her office. Bryce, her first patient today, was brought to see her because he has a rash on one of his legs. His other three legs are fine. Melissa asked Bryce if it itches, but Bryce didn't answer her question. She also noticed that Bryce's eyes were red, so she decided to take a closer look at them. Melissa prescribed some medicine for Bryce and said that he should be brought back to see her in two weeks.

Most likely, **who** is Melissa?

   A. an eye doctor
   B. a veterinarian
   C. a skin doctor

Cool Ears

People think of ears for hearing, but for elephants, they are also for cooling. Lots of blood vessels run through an elephant's ears. On a very hot day, an elephant can wet its ears and flap them. As the elephant flaps its ears, the blood flowing through all the blood vessels in the ears is cooled. The cooled blood then helps to cool the rest of the elephant as it circulates through the elephant's body. When Robert went to the zoo, he saw an elephant and thought, "Is that elephant okay? It isn't moving at all."

Most likely, **what** was the temperature when Robert was at the zoo?

   A. warm enough for shorts
   B. cool enough to wear a jacket
   C. hot enough to worry about sunstroke

Name _____   Date _____

Helpful Janet

The Phillips family all sat down at the table to eat dinner. Janet came by and gave everyone a glass of water. Then the people at the table told Janet what they wanted to eat for dinner. Ten minutes later, Janet came back holding a tray that had all the food. Janet checked in with the family every once in a while to see if they needed anything. When everyone was all finished eating, they gave Janet money.

Most likely, **who** is Janet?

A. a cook

B. a waitress

C. Mrs. Phillips

Missing Ingredient

Ernest was cooking a new chicken recipe for dinner when he realized that he was missing one ingredient. He stopped cooking so that he could go to the store to get onions. The grocery store was very close to his house. Ernest put on his sunglasses when he left the house because the sun was right in his eyes. When he walked out of the store, carrying the onions, it was dark out.

Most likely, **when** did Ernest go to the store?

A. at sunrise

B. at noon

C. at sunset

Name _____ **Date** _____

Book Hunting

As soon as Jasmine walked in, she saw books everywhere she looked. Jasmine walked to where the chapter books were because she was looking for a specific one to get for her friend's birthday. After looking for fifteen minutes, Jasmine asked a lady to help her find the book. The lady showed Jasmine where it was, and then Jasmine took the book to the counter. Jasmine couldn't wait to give it to her friend.

Most likely, **where** is Jasmine?

A. at a library

B. at school

C. at a bookstore

Quick Quiz

Mr. Thomas was calling on different students. "Texas," he said to Jeremiah. "Austin," Jeremiah replied. "New York," he said to Tory. "Albany," Tory replied. "Illinois," he said to Judy. "Chicago," replied Judy. "I'm sorry," the teacher told Judy. "Try that again."

Most likely, **what** is Mr. Thomas doing?

A. asking each student to name the capital of a state

B. asking each student to name a city that he or she has visited

C. asking each student to name the most popular city in a state

Name _____ **Date** _____

Return of the Monkeys

Whenever Tess and her dad go to the movie theater, they always go to the early showing. Tickets are usually cheaper for the early showtimes than for the later showtimes. Then, if it is early enough, they go out to lunch afterwards. Today, Tess and her dad are going to watch *Return of the Monkeys* at the theater. Tess wants to go out for pizza when it's over.

Most likely, **when** are Tess and her dad going to watch the movie?
- **A.** at 3:00 p.m.
- **B.** at 10:00 a.m.
- **C.** at 12:00 p.m.

Tiny Dots

French painter Georges Seurat didn't paint in long brush strokes. Instead, he painted tiny dots of color. Seurat's most famous painting is *A Sunday on La Grande Jatte*. The painting is more than ten feet across and almost seven feet high. It is estimated that Seurat made his painting with more than 3.5 million dots of paint! If you stand close to the painting, it looks like random dots of paint. If you stand a few feet away, you can see people and dogs picnicking at a park that is by the water. When Lance and Reagan went to the Art Museum, Lance said to Reagan, "A second grader could make this picture. It's only a bunch of dots."

Most likely, **where** were Lance and Reagan?
- **A.** very close to the painting
- **B.** a few feet away from the painting
- **C.** in the back of the room

Name _____ **Date** _____

Painting Dolphins

Michael is a very creative person. He is interested in dolphins and is always studying them for his paintings. Michael wants to make sure that the dolphins he paints look exactly like real dolphins. He has done several paintings of dolphins and has even made a sculpture of a dolphin. Michael sells his work to other people. They hang the paintings in their homes.

Most likely, **who** is Michael?

A. a scientist
B. a dolphin trainer
C. an artist

Under the Sea

Frank and Molly zipped up their wetsuits and jumped with all their gear into the water. On their backs, they had oxygen tanks which were connected by hoses to small breathing devices that were in their mouths. Frank and Molly stayed underwater for about thirty minutes without coming up to the surface. They saw lots of colorful fish swimming close to them. They even saw a giant clam that was over one foot wide! Both Frank and Molly wondered if a giant pearl was inside. They also wished that they had an underwater camera to take pictures of all that they were seeing.

Most likely, **who** are Frank and Molly?

A. pearl divers
B. photographers
C. scuba divers

New Furniture

Grandpa Bob bought new furniture for his twin granddaughters' bedroom. Holly and Polly were very excited when it was delivered. They helped their parents put everything together. That night, Polly stared at the bottom of Holly's bed. When Holly sat up in the morning, she almost hit her head on the ceiling. "I'm sure I'll get used to this soon enough," said Holly as she climbed down.

Most likely, **what** furniture did Grandpa Bob buy?

A. two twin-sized beds

B. a bunk bed

C. a tall dresser

Hungry Man

After basketball practice, Damian was hungry and tired. He opened up the refrigerator and took out some leftovers. After warming up the food, Damian ate it in less than two minutes. He put his head down when he finished and was asleep within seconds.

Most likely, **where** is Damian?

A. in his kitchen

B. in the school cafeteria

C. in a restaurant

Name _____ **Date** _____

Birthday Lunch

Skylar was driving with her mom to her grandma's house. Skylar's mom told her that her grandma wanted to take her out to lunch for her birthday. When Skylar opened the front door, her entire family jumped out from behind the furniture and shouted. This almost made Skylar fall backwards. "I guess I'm not going out to lunch with Grandma after all," said Skylar laughing.

Most likely, **how** did Skylar feel?
- **A.** upset
- **B.** surprised
- **C.** nervous

Collecting Coins

Chile is a country in South America. In 2008, the mint in Chile released 50-peso coins. Late in 2009, people noticed something about the coins. The word Chile was spelled wrong! Instead of C-H-I-L-E, the coins had C-H-I-I-E stamped on them! Like other people, Vicente began to look carefully at his 50-peso coins. He didn't want to spend them. He wanted to save them in hopes that they would become collectors' items. He hoped that one day they would be worth more than 50 pesos.

Most likely, **when** did Vicente begin to look carefully at his 50-peso coins?
- **A.** November 2008
- **B.** February 2009
- **C.** December 2009

Name _____ **Date** _____

Something Shiny

Charlotte was watching the magician at the party very carefully. First, the magician showed the group the large, empty box. The magician stepped inside the box, and his assistant closed the lid and locked him in. A few seconds later, the box opened, and the magician stood up. Charlotte saw something shiny fall out of the magician's hands. The kids wondered how the magician had gotten out.

Most likely, **what** fell from the magician's hands?

   A. a key
   B. a coin
   C. a wand

Drum Lessons

Fred goes to school from 8:00 a.m. until 2:15 p.m. every day except Wednesday. On Wednesdays, the school day ends at noon. On Tuesdays, Fred has to rush to be at swim practice on time. Fred's mom signed him up for weekly drum lessons. The drum teacher said that his only openings were at 1:00 p.m. on weekdays. His weekend times were already taken.

Most likely, **when** will Fred have drum lessons?

   A. on Wednesdays
   B. on Mondays
   C. on Saturdays

Name _____ **Date** _____

Science Camp

The fifth graders are leaving for science camp next week. The teachers held a meeting for all the parents so that the parents could learn more about the trip. The teachers scheduled the meeting for a time when they thought most of the parents would be able to attend. The teachers told the parents that the students would be studying animals and hiking. The students would also be learning about astronomy and doing other fun things at the camp. The parents each got a list of things that the students should pack for the week.

Most likely, **when** was the meeting?

A. in the morning

B. at noon

C. in the evening

Cooling Off

The Quinn family went for a boat ride one summer afternoon. Everyone started to get hot, so Mr. Quinn stopped the boat, and everyone jumped into the water to cool off. After Violet jumped in, she said, "I love swimming in this water because it's not salty!"

Most likely, **where** is the Quinn family?

A. in a lake

B. in an ocean

C. in a swimming pool

Name _____   **Date** _____

Traveling Back in Time

Diego and Autumn visited Japan. They liked seeing the busy city of Tokyo. It was very different than their small town in Hawaii. They got on their plane on Monday in order to return home. The flight home was estimated to take about eight hours. During the flight, when they looked down from the plane, they could see a huge ocean below them. When Diego and Autumn landed, it wasn't Monday any longer. It was Sunday! Diego said, "We crossed the International Date Line. We arrived sooner than we left!"

Most likely, **what** ocean did Diego and Autumn look down on while they were in the plane?

A. the Indian

B. the Pacific

C. the Atlantic

Lovely Languages

More people in the world speak Mandarin Chinese than any other language. One of the places Mandarin Chinese is spoken is China. Spanish is the second-most-spoken language. It is spoken in Spain and much of the Americas. English is third. England, the United States, and Canada are all English-speaking countries. Hindi is fourth, and one place it is spoken is India. Arabic is fifth. Arabic is spoken in many Middle Eastern countries. It is also spoken in North Africa. Karan said, "I grew up in India. I didn't move to the United States until I was in my twenties."

Most likely, Karan can speak **what** languages?

A. Hindi and the world's second-most-spoken language

B. the world's third and fourth most common languages

C. English and the world's most spoken language

Name _____ **Date** _____

Save Your Work

When typing on a computer, you can lose everything you have typed if you do not save your work. Sean was typing his report. He was halfway done typing it when he decided to take a break. Sean closed the program and never pressed the save button.

Predict the outcome.

   A. Sean will start typing where he left off.

   B. Sean will lose everything that he already typed.

   C. Sean will finish typing tomorrow.

Free Eggs

Liz has pet chickens that she keeps in her backyard. The chickens lay a lot of eggs, so she doesn't have to buy eggs very often. Liz likes having chickens because her favorite breakfast food is eggs. Whenever the chickens lay eggs, Liz cooks eggs for the next morning's breakfast. Liz collected four eggs from the chicken coop today.

Predict the outcome.

   A. In the morning, Liz will sell the eggs.

   B. Liz will buy eggs from the grocery store.

   C. In the morning, Liz will make eggs for breakfast.

Name _____ **Date** _____

No Misspelled Words

Sometimes when Wesley doesn't know how to spell a word, he asks his mom how to spell it. She never tells him how. She always says the first two letters and then tells him to look it up in the dictionary. When Wesley was writing his essay at home, he didn't remember how to spell the word *definitely*. He didn't want any misspelled words in his essay.

Predict the outcome.

   A. Wesley's mom will tell him how to spell the word.

   B. Wesley will look up how to spell the word in a dictionary.

   C. Wesley will just guess how to spell the word.

Shoe Issues

Maria has a shoe organizer in her closet where she puts all her shoes. The organizer can hold up to 10 pairs of shoes. Maria has eight pairs of shoes. She has two pairs of tennis shoes, two pairs of sandals, one pair of boots, two pairs of dress shoes, and one pair of flip flops. Maria received another pair of tennis shoes for her birthday.

Predict the outcome.

   A. Maria's organizer won't have space for the new shoes.

   B. Maria will put the new shoes under her bed.

   C. Maria will put the new shoes in her shoe organizer.

Name _____   **Date** _____

Island Bound

A large crowd of people waited by Gate 16 in a Nevada airport. They were waiting for the airplane crew to finish preparing the plane for their flight. Everyone was headed to Hawaii. Most of them were going on vacation, a few were going for work, and some were just going back home. Finally, they heard someone say that they could get in line to board the plane.

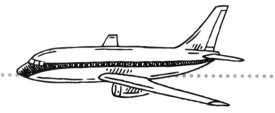

Predict the outcome.
   A. The plane will be full of people.
   B. The plane tickets will not cost a lot.
   C. The plane will fly to Nevada.

Please, Do Not Touch

The golden poison frog may be the most poisonous of any living animal. The frog is sometimes known simply as a golden frog or a golden dart frog. It lives in the rainforests of Colombia. The frog stores poison in its skin glands, so its skin is coated in poison. When scientists study these frogs, they have to wear thick gloves. Some native people coat their darts with the frog's poison. The tiniest amount of the poison is enough to kill a very large animal. Several scientists recently went to Colombia to study the golden frog.

Predict the outcome.
   A. A scientist will coat his darts with the frog's poison.
   B. A scientist will protect his hands before he handles the frog.
   C. A scientist will go to the rainforests in Costa Rica.

Name _____ **Date** _____

Piles of Papers

For Earth Day, Camden's class collected newspapers for recycling. For the past two months, all the students had saved their newspapers. Other students in other classes had saved their newspapers, too. All the students turned in their newspapers on Earth Day. A man from the recycling center came to the school and picked up the newspapers.

Predict the outcome.

 A. The newspapers will be recycled into something new.
   B. The man will read the newspapers.
   C. The man will print a story in the newspaper about recycling.

Staying Fit

Roman and Jenny like to exercise, but they are so busy that they only get a chance to exercise every once in a while. Roman and Jenny like lifting weights, doing push-ups, and running. Their muscles are always sore the next day. Later today, Roman and Jenny are going to exercise for the first time in three months. They are meeting friends to lift weights and then run around the track.

Predict the outcome.

   A. Roman and Jenny will not be able to lift the weights.
   B. Roman and Jenny will feel sick after exercising.
   C. Roman and Jenny will be sore tomorrow.

Name _____ **Date** _____

Ready to Rock

Lexi was saving her money to buy a guitar. She needed about $100. Lexi really wants to learn how to play the guitar. Lexi's parents told her that if she saved up enough money to buy a guitar, they would pay for the guitar lessons. A few months later, Lexi had earned $70 by mowing lawns and babysitting. She had also received $30 in birthday money.

Predict the outcome.
   A. Lexi will buy a guitar with her money.
   B. Lexi's parents will buy her a guitar.
   C. Lexi will get a guitar for her birthday.

Family Photos

Everyone in the Webb family dressed in nice clothes and went to the park. Mr. and Mrs. Webb hired a photographer to take their family pictures. The Webbs are going to frame the best picture and give it to Grandma Webb as a gift. The Webbs all thought the picture of them on the big rock was good, but they decided the picture of them by the pond turned out the best.

Predict the outcome.
   A. The Webbs will frame the picture of them by the big rock.
   B. The Webbs will frame the picture of them by the pond.
   C. The Webbs will hire a photographer for Grandma Webb.

Name _____ **Date** _____

Bad Rash

Max found out that he was allergic to almonds when, two years ago, he ate a candy bar with almonds in it. Max broke out in a bad rash, and it became hard for him to breathe. Doctors told Max to never eat almonds again. Now, Max always makes sure there aren't any almonds in his food. When Max got a treat bag from a party he went to, he found that it was filled with candy, a yo-yo, and three pencils.

Predict the outcome.

  A. Max will not use anything that was in the bag.
  B. Max will eat all of the candy without checking it.
  C. Max will not eat any candy that has almonds in it.

Tongue-Twister

Ms. Yoo said to her class, "What is a tongue-twister? A tongue-twister is something that is really hard to say fast several times. I am going to write a tongue-twister on the board. Some people say that this tongue-twister is one of the most difficult to say in the world." Ms. Yoo wrote "The sixth sick sheik's sixth sheep's sick" on the board. Then she asked the students to read what she wrote.

Predict the outcome.

  A. The students will agree that what Ms. Yoo wrote is a difficult tongue-twister.
  B. The students will agree that what Ms. Yoo wrote is not a difficult tongue-twister.
  C. Only a few of the students will agree that what Ms. Yoo wrote is a difficult tongue-twister.

Name _____ **Date** _____

Swimming Safely

Nadia does not know how to swim without help. Whenever she is in a pool, she always stays in the shallow end where her feet can touch the bottom. To get near the deep end, she has to wear a life jacket. Nadia's parents recently enrolled her in private swimming lessons. She practices swimming every Monday and Wednesday.

Predict the outcome.

    A. Nadia will only learn how to swim in a life jacket.

    B. Nadia will always wear a life jacket when swimming.

    C. Nadia will learn how to swim after some swimming lessons.

Finding Volume

Andre was learning about volume in math class. He learned that to calculate the volume of a box, you have to multiply its length times its width times its height. Andre was asked to calculate the volume of a box that is 10 inches long and 4 inches wide. Andre raised his hand to ask a question.

Predict the outcome.

    A. Andre will ask what the box is for.

    B. Andre will ask what the height of the box is.

    C. Andre will ask if he can use a calculator.

Name _____ **Date** _____

Remote Ruckus

Alan and his sister Rachel were fighting over the TV remote. Their mother told them to leave the remote alone. She said that if they didn't stop fighting over it, they would not be allowed to watch TV. Five minutes later, Alan and Rachel started fighting over the remote again.

Predict the outcome.

A. The children's mother will turn off the TV.

B. The children's mother will change the channel for them.

C. The children's mother will give Alan and Rachel each a remote.

Alice's Animals

Alice has a lot of family members who live nearby. She often earns money by taking care of their various pets. She will walk their dogs, and she will make sure their pets are fed and watered if the family members leave on vacation. Alice gets two dollars every time she walks a dog and one dollar every time she puts out food and water for a dog, cat, or other small animal. This weekend, Alice will walk her aunt and uncle's three dogs two times each. For two days, she will also put out food and water for her grandma's cat.

Predict the outcome.

A. Alice will earn fourteen dollars.

B. Alice will earn forty dollars.

C. Alice will earn four hundred dollars.

Name _____ **Date** _____

Two Brains Are Better Than One

Cole and Mariah were doing their math homework together. They had to do five word problems and twenty multiplication facts. The word problems were all about money. Cole and Mariah finished all the word problems and ten of the multiplication facts.

Predict what will happen.

 A. Cole and Mariah will do ten more word problems.
 B. Cole and Mariah will do five more multiplication facts.
 C. Cole and Mariah will do ten more multiplication facts.

Long Drive South

Jordan and Allie started in Canada. They were going to drive south all the way to Mexico. Driving through Montana, they saw a lot of elk. Allie told Jordan that Montana has the largest migratory elk herd in the 50 states. In Wyoming, they didn't see many people. Jordan told Allie that out of all 50 states, Wyoming had the smallest population.

Predict what will happen.

 A. Jordan and Allie will go through Georgia next.
 B. Jordan and Allie will go through Colorado next.
 C. Jordan and Allie will go through Vermont next.

Name _____ **Date** _____

Watching the Clock

Mark has baseball practice every Tuesday at 4:00 p.m. He always walks to the park for practice. It takes him 15 minutes to get there. He knows that if he leaves his house at 3:45 p.m., he will be right on time. This afternoon, Mark left the house at 3:55 p.m.

Predict the outcome.

   A. Mark will probably be right on time.
   B. Mark will probably be late.
   C. Mark will probably be early.

Not Microwave Safe

Tess often uses the microwave to heat food. Her parents have told her many times that it's not safe to microwave anything with metal in it. Metal can create sparks when microwaved. Tess wanted to warm up a bowl of chili. She microwaved the chili for one minute, stirred it with a metal spoon, and then microwaved it for another minute. Tess forgot to take the spoon out of the bowl before microwaving it again.

Predict the outcome.

   A. The metal spoon will create sparks.
   B. The metal spoon will melt.
   C. The chili will not taste good.

Name _____ **Date** _____

Online Invitation

Patrick was typing an email to his friends. He wanted to invite his friends to his birthday party. In the email, Patrick wrote the date and the time of the party. As Patrick was finishing the email invitation, the power went out, and the computer turned off.

Predict the outcome.
A. The email invitation will not get sent.
B. The lights in Patrick's room will turn on.
C. Patrick will cancel his birthday party.

Crazy Hair Day

Today is "Crazy Hair Day" at Paloma's school. This morning, Paloma sprayed her brown hair with blue hair coloring. Then she put her hair in ten different ponytails. The directions on the spray can said that the color will wash off easily. After school, Paloma is going straight to the shower in order to wash her hair.

Predict the outcome.
A. At school tomorrow morning, Paloma's hair will be brown.
B. At school tomorrow morning, Paloma's hair will be blue.
C. At school tomorrow morning, Paloma's hair will be dirty.

Name _____   **Date** _____

A Different Point of View

The local theater was putting on a play. It was called *Cinderella from the Stepsister's Point of View*. Paul and April had a lot of friends who were part of the cast. Their friends had told Paul and April that the play was very funny. They said that just the costumes made them smile. They also said it was very amusing to see Cinderella played as "sickly sweet." Paul and April got tickets for the front row.

Predict the outcome.

   A. Paul and April will not be able to view the costumes well from their seats.
   B. Paul and April will feel sick about the way Cinderella is played.
   C. Paul and April will be entertained when they watch their friends.

Rapping and Rhyming

Marshall really liked rap music. He often composed his own lyrics. Most of all, Marshall liked composing songs that rhymed. Every Monday, Marshall would think of one line. He would add an additional rhyming line every day for the rest of the week. Then, on the following Monday, he would start a new song or write another section that had a different rhyme. One Monday, Marshall wrote, "Only a fool stays away from school." On Tuesday, he wrote, "Using your brain is always cool."

Predict the outcome.

   A. Marshall will write, "You can become an astronaut if you do your homework," on Tuesday.
   B. Marshall will write, "Keep it cool and run away so you can play in the snow," on Wednesday.
   C. Marshall will write, "Knowledge is a jewel of a tool," on Wednesday.

Name _____ Date _____

Birthday Wishes

Mia, Marilyn, Kristy, and Leslie are all best friends. Whenever it is one of their birthdays, the other friends like to see who can be the first one to say "Happy Birthday" to the birthday girl. When it was Mia's birthday, she got phone calls early in the morning. Tomorrow is Leslie's birthday.

Predict the outcome.
- **A.** Leslie will get phone calls early in the morning.
- **B.** Leslie will call Kristy early in the morning.
- **C.** Marilyn will call Mia early in the morning.

Pizza Night

Lou's dad, Carl, asked Lou to order two pizzas for dinner. Carl said that Lou could order any type of pizza that he wanted, but at least one had to be cheese. Lou told his dad that he needed the phone number. Carl told him that the number was 469-153. Lou knows that there are seven digits in every phone number.

Predict the outcome.
- **A.** Lou will order two supreme pizzas with extra cheese.
- **B.** Lou will need to know the missing digit before he phones.
- **C.** Lou will eat pieces from each pizza he orders.

Name _____ **Date** _____

Shedding Skin

We grow new skin cells and shed old skin cells all the time. Snakes do the same, but they do it a bit differently. We shed our old skin cells constantly and in small amounts. Snakes do it all at once, shedding their skin in one continuous sheet. Younger snakes that are still growing may shed their skin every few weeks. Adult snakes may shed their skin only two times a year. When a snake is ready to shed, it will often seek out a rough surface to help rub the old skin off. When Aubrey and Doug went to the zoo, they saw a snake begin to rub against some stones resting along the enclosure wall. One child started to cry. "The snake is trying to get out," he said.

Predict the outcome.

   A. The snake will shed its skin in small amounts.
   B. The snake will shed its skin in one continuous sheet.
   C. Aubrey and Doug will tell the zookeeper that the snake is trying to get out.

Family Movie Night

Every Friday, the Lee family has "family movie night" at home. Mr. Lee always rents or downloads a new movie they haven't seen before. Then he makes popcorn for his children that they can eat while they watch the movie. The children are always curious to find out what movie they are going to watch. Today is Friday.

Predict the outcome.

   A. Mr. Lee will take his kids to the movie theater.
   B. Mr. Lee will rent or download his kids' favorite movie.
   C. Mr. Lee will make popcorn and rent or download a new movie.

Runaway Meatball

Scott's family was having spaghetti and meatballs for dinner. First, Scott scooped noodles onto his plate. Then, he put five meatballs on top of the noodles. Next, he covered the noodles and the meatballs with pasta sauce. As Scott mixed everything together, a meatball fell off his plate and rolled onto the kitchen floor.

Predict the outcome.
A. There will be sauce on the floor.
B. There will be noodles on the floor.
C. The floor will be clean.

Fast Bike

Karen said, "I was riding my bike at 12 miles per hour. I was going 12 miles per hour, but I managed to pass two bikes that were going 15 miles per hour. I even passed a car that was going 30 miles per hour! I am telling the truth." When Isaac asked Karen if there was anything special about her bike, Karen told him that her bike was ordinary. It wasn't special at all.

Predict the outcome.
A. Isaac will tell Karen that there must be something special about her bike.
B. Isaac will tell Karen that she was incorrect about the speed of the two bikes and the car she passed.
C. Isaac will tell Karen that she was riding her bike in the opposite direction of the two bikes and the car she passed.

Name _____ **Date** _____

The **main idea** of a story is what it's mostly about. Often, the title of the story gives us a hint about the main idea.

Below, write four sentences: two with *movie titles* and two with *book titles*.

Given the title of the movie or book, tell what you would expect the main idea to be. Then tell what you discovered. Your titles and sentences can be serious or silly. All your sentences must follow the sentence structure in the example.

Twisted Titles

Example:

When I went to see the movie Danger on the Atlantic, *I thought it would be about a ship in a storm. Consequently, I was shocked when I learned it was about knitting.*

Make sure to underline book titles and movie titles.

Movie Titles

1. When _____

_____.

Consequently, _____.

2. _____

_____

_____

Book Titles

3. _____

_____

_____

4. _____

_____

_____

Name _____ **Date** _____

Think about the laws in this country. If you had to write about laws, you could write about so many things! You could write about the history of the laws, how they are written, how they are enforced, and what happens if you don't obey them. You are going to write about laws, but you will have a specific **main idea**. Your main idea will be to give an example of one good law and one silly law. Knowing your main idea will help you stay organized.

You will need an additional sheet of paper to complete this assignment.

Law and Order

> **First paragraph:** *Introduce your topic by explaining what a law is and what you will be writing about. Next, give an example of one good law. Tell how this law helps people. What might happen if we didn't have this law?*
>
> **Second paragraph:** *Pick one of the silly laws from the list below. Tell how you think this law came about. (Make your story as wild and fun as you want!) Then tell if you think this law is still needed today.*

Silly Laws

- In Missouri, you cannot drive down the highway with an uncaged bear in the car.
- In Farmington, Connecticut, cows have the same rights on roads as motorists do.
- In Fargo, North Dakota, it is illegal to fall asleep with your shoes on.
- In St. Croix, Wisconsin, women are not allowed to wear anything red.
- In Boston, Massachusetts, it is illegal to take a bath unless ordered to by a doctor.

_____

_____

_____

_____

_____

_____

_____

Name _____ Date _____

Inside the Head of an Astronaut

There is a lot to say about space exploration, but you are going to focus on one little part.

On July 20, 1969, Neil Armstrong and Edwin "Buzz" Aldrin made history as the first two men to ever walk on the moon. While these two astronauts explored the surface of the moon, Mike Collins stayed in the spaceship. He circled around the dark side of the moon, which means he had no radio contact with Earth or the other astronauts. No one in the world had ever been more alone than he was. Collins didn't know if the moon landing craft would be able to make it back to his ship. He didn't know if the timing would work out. He didn't know if he would have to return alone. He didn't even know if he'd be able to return at all.

Imagine you are Mike Collins. Write a paragraph in which you share all your thoughts as you wait to pick up your two fellow astronauts on the moon. Use information from the paragraph above when you write.

Remember to use the word "I" because you are writing as Mike Collins.

_____

_____

_____

_____

_____

_____

_____

_____

_____

_____

_____

Name _____   **Date** _____

Imagine you are a newspaper reporter. You write for an online newspaper, and the picture below is part of your story. Think of a caption that can go underneath the picture. The caption should be short and should sum up the action. The caption should fit with the **main idea** of the story.

Breaking News

_____

_____

Now, write a paragraph in which you explain more about what is going on in the picture. Use your imagination to fill in details about **where**, **when**, **what**, **why**, and **how**.

Include at least one quote in your story. When you quote a person, you must put their words in quotation marks.

> *Example:*
>
> *Jason told the judge, "I don't think the boy meant to ride his skateboard over my foot."*

_____

_____

_____

_____

_____

Name _____   **Date** _____

Look around the classroom and take a good look at your friends. Note the differences and the similarities between each person.

Now, write five sentences about you and these friends. In each sentence, describe how two people in your class are similar and how they are different. You can use two different people for each sentence if you want.

The Same but Different

Example:

Lexie and Marisa are both wearing knee-high boots today, but Lexie's boots, in contrast to Marisa's, are dark brown instead of tan.

1. _____ are both _____,

   but _____, in contrast to _____,

   _____.

2. _____

   _____

   _____

3. _____

   _____

   _____

4. _____

   _____

   _____

5. _____

   _____

   _____

Name _____ **Date** _____

Food Finders

Think of any supermarket. Foods are not placed randomly on the shelves. They are grouped together. Also, foods are placed strategically. You might impulsively buy a drink or a snack as you are checking out. Food products advertised to children are placed so children can see and grab them. More expensive brands are seldom on the bottom or top shelf.

Close your eyes and visualize your local grocery store. Take a moment and "walk" through the store, looking at the different items on the shelves and the various displays. Now, write down <u>fifteen</u> details about this store, describing what you might see and where you would see it. Your details can be general ("The produce is on the left side of the store.") or very specific ("My favorite cereal, *Fruity Sugar Blast,* is in the middle of the cereal aisle next to *Chocolate Tasty-Ohs.*").

Make sure to write complete sentences.

1. _____
2. _____
3. _____
4. _____
5. _____
6. _____
7. _____
8. _____
9. _____
10. _____
11. _____
12. _____
13. _____
14. _____
15. _____

Name _____ **Date** _____

The Shape of Poetry

You are going to write a shape poem. First, think of a shape. Your shape can be a chair, snowman, circle, piece of fruit, shoe—anything you want! Then, think of some lines that describe *details about your shape* or *how the shape makes you feel*. Your poem does not have to rhyme!

Lightly sketch your shape in each of the boxes below. Lightly pencil in the lines you wrote. Your lines can follow the shape's outline, or they can fill up the inside of the shape. Adjust your letter size if you need to. Once you know about how things will fit, make a final copy in darker print. Erase the shape lines so only the words remain.

Inside the Shape

My
snowy friend
You visit just
once a year
Let's dance and play
In the cold winter sun
Before warm skies
Take you home

Outline the Shape

One day I will · Climb out of · This box and · Stand on the outside · And look in

After creating a final draft, staple a copy of everyone's poems together to make a class poetry book.

Name _____ **Date** _____

Talking Pictures

Sometimes we need to look closer at a picture in order to notice all the details. Look carefully at the picture above for as many details as you can. In the spaces below, write four details about what you see.

1. _____

2. _____

3. _____

4. _____

Now, use the details above to create a dialogue between the two people in the picture. Make up your own names for the two people. Your dialogue needs to be a minimum of ten lines. You will need an additional sheet of paper to complete this assignment.

In this activity, you do not need to use quotation marks because you are using a colon to introduce each line of dialogue.

Example:

Billy: *Can you believe . . .*

Tommy: *No I can't, but . . .*

_____

_____

_____

_____

Name _____ **Date** _____

Sometimes the writer of a story does not tell you exactly where a character is. You often have to figure it out from the way the character acts or from descriptive details.

Destination Unknown

Think of four different locations. They can be general (like a desert, ocean, or continent) or very specific (at your school, your bedroom, or at a famous building). Then write two or three sentences about each location. Don't name the location in your sentence! Make your reader figure it out.

> *Example:*
>
> *The hot air burned his nose, and wherever he looked, endless hills of yellow sand silently mocked him. The towel he had wrapped around his face was drenched with sweat. He started to regret not telling anyone where he was going.*

Location 1: _____

_____

_____

Location 2: _____

_____

_____

Location 3: _____

_____

_____

Location 4: _____

_____

_____

Pass your paper to four of your classmates. In the margins, have each of them write what location they think you were writing about. Let them know if they were correct or not. *(The location in the example above was a desert in Africa or the Middle East.)*

Name _____   Date _____

Imagine that you are a drop of water. Write a paragraph sharing your inner thoughts. Make it sound as though you are on an amazing journey. Your journey can be fun, exciting, or even dangerous, but *don't reveal that you are a drop of water until the very last line.* Try to keep your true identity a secret until the end of your story.

The Amazing Journey

Example **beginning** sentences:

Look at all of these beautiful fish!

Help, I'm falling!

I woke up this morning inside a cloud.

Example **ending** sentences:

As soon as this snow melts, I can finally become a water droplet again.

Life is always exciting when you're a drop of water!

_____

_____

_____

_____

_____

_____

_____

_____

Read the first part of your paragraph out loud. Put a lot of emotion into your voice. Could someone be unsure of the narrator's identity if they didn't read the entire paragraph?

Name _____ **Date** _____

Look at the pictures below. You are not told when each of the pictures was taken, but most likely, you can tell. For each picture, write a paragraph explaining from what time period you think the pictures were taken. As you write your paragraphs, include details from the pictures that helped you come to your conclusions.

Frozen in Time

_____
_____
_____
_____
_____
_____
_____
_____

_____
_____
_____
_____
_____
_____
_____
_____
_____

Name _____   **Date** _____

Two hard words to read are *repugnant* and *delectable*.

When something is *repugnant*, it is offensive, obnoxious, shocking, distasteful, and gross.

When something is *delectable*, it is delicious, enjoyable, delightful, and highly pleasing.

Imagine you are teaching someone what these two hard words mean. Without stating their definitions, write three sentences each (six in all) using each word.

Two of the sentences have been started for you.

Building Your Vocabulary

1. It was the most *repugnant* meal I had ever been served because _____

_____

2. _____

_____

3. _____

_____

4. The most *delectable* meal I can remember was _____

_____

5. _____

_____

6. _____

_____

Do you think someone could figure out what *repugnant* and *delectable* mean after reading your sentences? How?

_____

_____

_____

Name _____ **Date** _____

A **fact** is a thing that has happened. A fact is true.

An **opinion** is what you think.

Speak Your Mind

It is a fact that most zoos house a variety of animals from different parts of the world. Some people believe these animals should be living in their natural habitat. Other people feel that the animals in zoos are safe, happy, and well cared for. Do you think animals should be kept in zoos or left alone to live in the wild? Explain your answer.

Construct a paragraph using facts and opinions to support your answer.

Write a paragraph in which sentences **one** and **two** start out like this:

It is a fact that zoos have _____

_____.

It is a fact that people feel strongly about _____

_____.

Your **third** sentence starts out like this:

It is my opinion that _____

_____.

Sentences **four**, **five**, and **six** (more if you want) should tell *why* you think so. Defend your opinion! Give reasons why your opinion is a good one!

_____

_____

_____

_____.

The **last** sentence should start out like this:

In conclusion, I feel that zoos should _____

_____.

On a separate piece of paper, combine the sentences from above to form a complete paragraph supporting your opinion.

Name _____ **Date** _____

Write a dialogue between two people who are discussing food. In your dialogue, have each person say one **fact** and one **opinion** about a food.

When you write, pick your own names.

Underline the facts. Put [brackets] around the opinions.

Food Talk

Example:

Kellie: [Watermelon used to be so much fun to eat!] What happened?

Kyle: I agree! [Spitting out the seeds is the best part!]

Kellie: Would you believe that less than ten percent of watermelons sold last year had seeds?

Kyle: Kids could choke on the seeds, so [maybe it's a good thing the seeds are disappearing.]

_____

_____

_____

_____

_____

_____

_____

_____

_____

_____

Pick two classmates to read your dialogue to the class. Have the class identify which sentences are facts and which are opinions.

Name _____ **Date** _____

Is the story in the box below true? Write a paragraph in which you discuss whether or not this story is factual, and why. Make sure you support your answer with **facts**.

Your paragraph should include transition words (such as *additionally* and *furthermore*) and should include a strong concluding sentence. Your final sentence should remind the reader your **opinion** about how true the story is. You may finish the final sentence below or you can make up a completely new one.

Believe It or Not?

> *The Lincoln Memorial is in Lincoln, Nebraska. It is a statue of President George Washington standing by his white horse. The statue is made out of gold, and to get to it, one has to go down 49 steps because Lincoln was the 49th president. The words "I have a dream" are carved on the walls around the statue because those words came from Lincoln's most famous speech. The memorial was designed by Walt Disney.*

_____

_____

_____

_____

_____

_____

_____

_____

_____

__It is my opinion that the story is__ _____

_____

_____

Name _____ **Date** _____

Imagine that when you wake up in the morning, you will have a super power that will last for exactly one year. You will either have the ability to fly, or you will be able to turn invisible whenever you want. Which super power would you prefer? Think carefully about all the good (and bad!) things that could happen with both super powers. Remember, the powers only last for one year!

A Super Year

Write a paragraph in which you tell which power you would choose and why. Give at least *three* examples of things you might do with your super power.

Your paragraph has been started for you.

If I could choose to be invisible or have the power to fly for one year, it is a fact that I would choose _____. **It is my opinion that this is the best choice because** _____

_____.

_____

_____

_____

_____

_____

_____

_____

_____

_____

_____

_____

_____

_____

Name _____   **Date** _____

Finding Cause and Effect

Read this sentence:

When I heard that the music store was offering free drum lessons, I immediately called to learn more information.

When I heard that the music store was offering free drum lessons is the **cause**. It is **why** it happened.

I immediately called to learn more information is the **effect**. It is **what** happened.

Practice writing the part of the sentence that is the **cause**.

1. When _____, I decided to go outside and celebrate.

2. _____, so I held my breath and tried to stay as quiet as possible.

Practice writing the part of the sentence that is the **effect**.

1. After seeing the orangutan in the front seat of my car, _____

   _____.

2. When I heard that I had to return the one-million-dollar prize, _____

   _____.

Now write two sentences of your own that each have a cause and an effect. <u>Underline</u> the cause. (Circle) the effect.

1. _____

   _____

2. _____

   _____

Name _____ **Date** _____

Think about manners and the importance of being polite. Now imagine a society in which no one has any manners and no one is polite. Write one paragraph in which you first explain what manners are and why they are helpful. Give examples of ways people can be polite. (Think of what we say, how we eat, how we dress, and how we behave.)

Missing Manners

Write a second paragraph in which you describe a scene where no one has manners. Your paragraph can be realistic, very imaginative, or funny. Be sure to end your paragraph with a strong concluding sentence.

_____

_____

_____

_____

_____

_____

_____

_____

_____

_____

_____

_____

_____

_____

_____

_____

_____

_____

_____

Name _____ **Date** _____

Waxing and Waning

All around the world, there are different myths about the moon. These myths each have a **cause** and an **effect**. The myths deal with the fact that the moon wanes (gets smaller) and waxes (gets bigger). This is the *effect*. The explanation about what makes the moon wax and wane is the *cause*. Some myths include 12 new moons per year. Other myths have an animal eating the same moon over and over.

Create your own myth about the moon. Explain why the moon waxes and wanes. Your myth can be set in ancient or present times. It can involve people or animals. Be creative!

_____

_____

_____

_____

_____

_____

_____

_____

_____

_____

_____

_____

_____

_____

_____

_____

Name _____ **Date** _____

Talking Animals

Many famous books include talking animals. For example, in *Charlotte's Web*, a spider talks to a pig. In *The Cat in the Hat*, a talking cat befriends two children. A snake talks to Harry Potter in *Harry Potter and the Sorcerer's Stone*. Talking animals (and their effect on the other characters) is one of the tools an author can use to make a story more interesting and entertaining.

Write your own story that includes a talking animal. You pick what animal can talk and whom it can talk to. In your story, your talking animal must have an *effect* on the other characters or on the plot. You can make your story fantastic, realistic, or silly. Use your imagination and have fun!

_____

_____

_____

_____

_____

_____

_____

_____

_____

_____

_____

_____

_____

_____

_____

_____

_____

_____

Name _____   **Date** _____

While sitting in your bedroom one afternoon, an alien from another galaxy crawls in through your window and sits on the floor just inches from your feet. With a long green tentacle, it points to your cell phone and then to the sky outside. Thinking the alien needs to use your cell phone to make an important call, you hand over your phone. Within seconds, the alien is chewing on your phone and trying to swallow it! It must think eating the phone will enable it to send messages telepathically! It's up to you to show the alien how to properly use a mobile phone.

Alien Encounter

Think about all the steps that go into using a cell phone. Start from the very beginning—how to hold it, how to turn it on, and how to send and receive messages (voice and text). Teach it how to take a picture, too. Write down the steps in order. Make sure to use proper sequencing words such as **first**, **second**, **then**, **next**, **after**, and **finally**.

_____

_____

_____

_____

_____

_____

_____

_____

_____

_____

_____

_____

_____

_____

Name _____ **Date** _____

Think of *six* important events or milestones in your life. These events can be important for any reason, just as long as they are important memories to you. The events can be enjoyable memories, experiences that made you think a different way, or events that helped define who you are. One of these milestones should be the day you were born.

Memorable Milestones

In the space below, write down the events in sequential order. That means you are going to write them down in the order in which they happened. Use words like **first**, **second**, **third**, **next**, **following**, and **finally** in order to help your sentences flow.

_____

_____

_____

_____

_____

_____

_____

_____

_____

_____

_____

_____

_____

_____

On a separate piece of paper, write down your important events in a random order. Mix them up! Choose two or three events and share them with friends in your classroom. Are they able to put your events in the correct order?

Name _____ **Date** _____

When you write, these words and phrases help the reader know when things happened:

Cosmic Complications

> **first**, **second**, **third**, **before**,
> **previously**, **then**, **next**, **finally**,
> **after**, **in conclusion**, **soon after**,
> **after a short while**

Use at least *seven* of these words or phrases when you make up a story about traveling through space and encountering a problem. Your story can be realistic or silly. Underline the words you use from the list.

Example:

After passing Jupiter, I saw something strange on the left side of the spaceship. I decided to first turn the spaceship around and . . .

_____

_____

_____

_____

_____

_____

_____

_____

_____

_____

_____

_____

Name _____ **Date** _____

Look at the pictures. Think about what happened first, second, third, and last. Are the pictures in the correct order? Write a **1**, **2**, **3**, or **4** under each picture to show the correct order. Next, use these pictures to create a story, and write a paragraph explaining what happened.

Out of Order

_____

_____

_____

_____

_____

_____

_____

_____

_____

_____

Name _____ **Date** _____

A *herpetologist* studies frogs and snakes.

An *ichthyologist* studies fish and sharks.

An *entomologist* studies insects.

A *paleontologist* studies the fossils of ancient life.

A *zoologist* studies animals.

Name That Scientist!

Write three short paragraphs. Each paragraph will focus on a different scientist from above. In your paragraph, include the inner thoughts of the scientist as he or she is conducting research. Don't say what scientist the paragraph is about! Make your reader figure it out by the words you choose and by the actions of the scientist!

Example:

"I'm sure glad I wore my old clothes today because this place is filthy. Although I love my job, brushing away small pieces of rock and dirt out here in the hot desert sun can sometimes get quite unpleasant." (paleontologist)

Scientist 1: _____

_____

_____

_____

Scientist 2: _____

_____

_____

_____

Scientist 3: _____

_____

_____

_____

Read one of your paragraphs to your classmates. Could they tell which scientist your paragraph was about?

Name _____   Date _____

Common Phobias

Help Me, Doctor

Acrophobia is the fear of heights.

Agoraphobia is the fear of open spaces.

Arachnophobia is the fear of spiders.

Claustrophobia is the fear of enclosed spaces.

Triskaidekaphobia is the fear of the number thirteen.

Write one or two paragraphs pretending to have one of the phobias listed above. Write down what you would say to the doctor during your first appointment. Describe something (or several things!) that happened to you, and then describe in detail how you felt and how you reacted. You can make it exciting, funny, or sad.

Doctor, I have a problem. _____

_____

_____

_____

_____

_____

_____

_____

_____

_____

_____

_____

_____ ## Doctor, what is the matter with me?

Doctor's Diagnosis: _____

Name _____ **Date** _____

We often encounter math problems in our daily lives. Sometimes, a simple trip to the grocery store or a ride on a bus requires us to use math. Typically, when solving these daily problems, we either add, subtract, multiply, or divide.

On the lines below, create four word problems. Each word problem should require a different mathematic operation to solve: addition, subtraction, multiplication, or division. Write challenging (but realistic) problems, but don't say what operation is needed!

Math Is Everywhere

1. _____

_____

_____

2. _____

_____

_____

3. _____

_____

_____

4. _____

_____

_____

Read one of your problems out loud. Can the other students in your class infer which mathematic operation is needed to solve the problem?

Which operation is needed to solve the problem?

1: _____ 3: _____

2: _____ 4: _____

Name _____ **Date** _____

In the pictures below, you are not told what is going to happen next, but you can come up with some good ideas!

Write down a sentence or two in which you describe the scene. Then tell what is going to happen *next*.

Use your imagination when you write your sentences, and try your best to entertain the reader!

What Happens Next?

_____
_____
_____
_____
_____
_____
_____
_____
_____
_____

_____
_____
_____
_____
_____
_____
_____
_____

138

Name _____ **Date** _____

Children's stories often have wild and fun plots. There may be talking animals, amazing adventures, or even encounters with friendly wild things. Sometimes, the art in these books can be just as important as the words, adding to the excitement and enjoyment of the story. When developing a story, the author is usually thinking about both the illustrations and the words and how they will work together.

Picture Pages

In the space below and on additional pages, write a picture book for children. Because your book will be for a younger audience, you only need to write a few sentences per page. You may illustrate it if you want, but you must write a few sentences for each page about where the illustrations will go and what they will be of. Be specific!

Page 1: _____

_____

_____

Description of illustration: _____

_____

_____

_____

Page 2: _____

_____

_____

Description of illustration: _____

_____

_____

_____

Your book should be about **eight to ten pages long** (longer if you want). Use additional pages to finish the assignment.

Name _____ **Date** _____

In 2013, Diana Nyad swam from Cuba to Florida. Write a radio announcement/news report about this swim. Use the facts listed below to help you with your announcement. Write it as if you are watching the event. Don't let your listeners know whether or not she makes it until the very end! Keep them on the edge of their seats with suspense!

Sensational Swimmer

Facts

Distance: 110 miles
Date: September 2, 2013
Route: from Cuba to Florida
Age: 64 years old
Total time: 52 hours, 54 minutes, 18.6 seconds

Other details:
- It was her fifth attempt since 1978.
- She was swimming in treacherous waters.
- Her tongue and lips were swollen from exposure to the sun and seawater.
- She had cuts in her mouth from the mask she wore to protect her face from jellyfish.
- She swam without a shark cage.

The beginning and the end of your news report has been started for you. Use additional paper if necessary.

Good evening, ladies and gentlemen, my name is _____,

and I am reporting live from _____.

_____

_____

_____

_____

_____

_____

This is _____ **at Channel** ____ **signing off. Back to you in the studio.**

Practice saying your news report out loud. Can you make it sound interesting and suspenseful?

Common Core State Standards Correlations

Each activity in *Instant Reading Comprehension Practice* meets one or more of the following Common Core State Standards (© Copyright 2010. National Governors Association Center for Best Practices and Council of Chief State School Officers. All rights reserved.). For more information about the Common Core State Standards, go to *http://www.corestandards.org* or visit *http://www.teachercreated.com/standards*.

Reading: Literature	
Key Ideas and Details	**Pages**
ELA-Literacy.RL.5.1 Quote accurately from a text when explaining what the text says explicitly and when drawing inferences from the text.	81–95
ELA-Literacy.RL.5.2 Determine a theme of a story, drama, or poem from details in the text, including how characters in a story or drama respond to challenges or how the speaker in a poem reflects upon a topic; summarize the text.	7–8, 10–11, 13–20
Craft and Structure	**Pages**
ELA-Literacy.RL.5.4 Determine the meaning of words and phrases as they are used in a text, including figurative language such as metaphors and similes.	36–50
ELA-Literacy.RL.5.5 Explain how a series of chapters, scenes, or stanzas fits together to provide the overall structure of a particular story, drama, or poem.	56–80
Range of Reading and Level of Text Complexity	**Pages**
ELA-Literacy.RL.5.10 By the end of the year, read and comprehend literature, including stories, dramas, and poetry, at the high end of the grades 4–5 text complexity band independently and proficiently.	7–8, 10–11, 13–22, 24–25, 27–28, 30–31, 34, 36–50, 56–110
Reading: Informational Text	
Key Ideas and Details	**Pages**
ELA-Literacy.RI.5.2 Determine two or more main ideas of a text and explain how they are supported by key details; summarize the text.	6–9, 11–12, 16–18, 20
Craft and Structure	**Pages**
ELA-Literacy.RI.5.4 Determine the meaning of general academic and domain-specific words and phrases in a text relevant to a *grade 5 topic or subject area*.	38, 46, 49
ELA-Literacy.RI.5.5 Compare and contrast the overall structure (e.g., chronology, comparison, cause/effect, problem/solution) of events, ideas, concepts, or information in two or more texts.	57, 61, 63, 65, 71, 78
Integration of Knowledge and Ideas	**Pages**
ELA-Literacy.RI.5.8 Explain how an author uses reasons and evidence to support particular points in a text, identifying which reasons and evidence support which point(s).	51–55

Range of Reading and Level of Text Complexity	Pages
ELA-Literacy.RI.5.10 By the end of the year, read and comprehend informational texts, including history/social studies, science, and technical texts, at the high end of the grades 4–5 text complexity band independently and proficiently.	6–9, 11–12, 16–18, 20, 23, 26, 29, 31–35, 38, 46, 49, 51–55, 57, 61, 63, 65, 71, 78, 98

Reading: Foundational Skills

Phonics and Word Recognition	Pages
ELA-Literacy.RF.5.3 Know and apply grade-level phonics and word-analysis skills in decoding words.	6–110

Fluency	Pages
ELA-Literacy.RF.5.4 Read with sufficient accuracy and fluency to support comprehension.	6–110

Writing

Text Types and Purposes	Pages
ELA-Literacy.W.5.1 Write opinion pieces on topics or texts, supporting a point of view with reasons and information.	112, 121, 123, 125–126, 134
ELA-Literacy.W.5.2 Write informative/explanatory texts to examine a topic and convey ideas and information clearly.	111–112, 114–116, 119, 121–122, 127–128, 131–132
ELA-Literacy.W.5.3 Write narratives to develop real or imagined experiences or events using effective technique, descriptive details, and clear event sequences.	113, 118–120, 124, 127, 129–130, 133, 135–140

Production and Distribution of Writing	Pages
ELA-Literacy.W.5.4 Produce clear and coherent writing in which the development and organization are appropriate to task, purpose, and audience.	111–140

Range of Writing	Pages
ELA-Literacy.W.5.10 Write routinely over extended time frames (time for research, reflection, and revision) and shorter time frames (a single sitting or a day or two) for a range of discipline-specific tasks, purposes, and audiences.	111–140

Answer Key

Finding Main Ideas

Page 6
Super-Sized: B
Finding Balance: C

Page 7
New Kid in Town: B
The Appearance
   of Roy G. Biv: A

Page 8
Special Scoops: C
Legless Lizards: A

Page 9
Delicious Mix: B
First-Day Friends: C

Page 10
Sparky the Dog: B
Cleaning Lessons: A

Page 11
Vegetable Victory: A
Fast Wheels: C

Page 12
Eight Seconds: B
Love Your Planet: C

Page 13
Rocket Man: A
Backyard Bounty: C

Page 14
Surf's Up: C
In the Clouds: A

Page 15
Tower 32: A
Stuffed Pig: B

Page 16
Birthday Wishes: C
Ironman: B

Page 17
Aiming for the Stars: C
Hot Water: A

Page 18
Thick Skin: B
Icy Inspiration: B

Page 19
Kindness Matters: A
Open for Business: A

Page 20
Olympic Greatness: B
Favorite Riddles: C

Noting Details

Page 21
Center of the States: B
Fresh Fruit: A

Page 22
Early Riser: B
Giving Thanks: C

Page 23
Borrowed Books: C
Tuvalu: B

Page 24
Tax Not Included: C
Bake Me a Cake: A

Page 25
Lost in Translation: A
Out with the Old: B

Page 26
Fierce Fish: C
Different but United: A

Page 27
Leap Day: C
Game Night: C

Page 28
Family Night Out: A
Summer Down Under: B

Page 29
Writing a Letter: B
The Sleeping One: A

Page 30
Faith's Flute: B
Palomino Party: C

Page 31
State Reports: B
Larry Legend: A

Page 32
Take a Picture: C
Big Babies: A

Page 33
Read Across
   America Day: B
A Lot of Water: B

Page 34
Counting Steps: C
Family Menu: A

Page 35
BASE Jumping: C
Desert Survivors: A

Using Context Clues

Page 36
Generous Donation: A
Memorizing Moves: C

Page 37
Homework First: B
Foul Ball: B

Page 38
Jeans: C
Wacky Weather: A

Page 39
What Does It Say?: B
Tough Question: C

Page 40
Picky Eater: B
Wild Animal: A

Page 41
Wobbly Legs: A
Shark Food: C

Page 42
Zoo Trip: C
Pool Play: A

Page 43
Well-Prepared: C
Spider Snacks: B

Page 44
Learning about Lincoln: A
Spider on the Loose: B

Page 45
Jokes and Riddles: B
Dead End: A

Page 46
Free Diving: C
Double Prints: B

Page 47
Candy Calculations: B
Good Friends: A

Page 48
Perfect Pies: C
Whiz Kid: B

Page 49
Leftover Dogs: C
Late Fees: A

Page 50
Complicated Conversions: A
Unexpected Adventure: C

Identifying Facts and Opinions

Page 51
Germ-Free: A, C
Learning Fractions: B, C
Happy Fish: B, C
Four-Legged Friends: A, C
Beautiful Words: A, B
Venomous Kings: A, B

Page 52
Math Minute: A, C
Moon-Walking: B, C
A Lot of Feet: A, B
Beautiful Brides: A, C
Fifty Nifty States: A, B
Dangerous Dinner: B, C

Page 53
Honest Abe: B, C
Digital Mail: A, C
Seven Wonders: A, B
Colorful Opinions: A, C
Reduce and Reuse: B, C
Four Great Inventions: A, C

Page 54
Making Money: A, B
Wonderful Words: B, C
Different Angles: A, C
Four-Sided Fun: A, B
Math's Best Friend: A, B
The Dead Sea: B, C

Page 55
A Full Deck: A, C
Juice It Up: A, B
Changing Directions: B, C
Old Glory: B, C
Meet the Swiftlets: A, B
Island Life: A, C

Answer Key (cont.)

Finding Cause and Effect

Page 56
Spooky Sounds: A
Come Back, Ollie: C
Wrap Star: A

Page 57
Facing His Fears: B
Time for Tea: B
Living in Slow Motion: C

Page 58
Favorite Photo: A
Hidden Treasure: B
Bake Sale: B

Page 59
New Flavor: C
Too Hot!: C
Riddle Restlessness: A

Page 60
No Movie Tonight: A
Late-Night Snack: B
The Trouble with Texting: C

Page 61
Vote for Dane: B
Lock It Up: C
Google It: A

Page 62
Grandfather's Chest: A
Protecting the Planet: B
Chili Cook-Off: C

Page 63
A Peek Under the Sea: B
Library Day: A
Protecting the Paws: C

Page 64
Filling the Buckets: C
Camera-Shy: B
Adoption Day: A

Page 65
Rained Out: C
Celebrating Safely: A
Talking Eggs: B

Sequencing

Page 66
Getting Ready for Bed: C
Wooden Airplane: A

Page 67
Almost There: B
Crossword Support: C

Page 68
Rainy-Day Schedule: C
Heading East: A

Page 69
Pumpkin Makeover: B
Animal Reports: A

Page 70
Yard Work: B
Not the Same: A

Page 71
Hostage Negotiators: C
The Quiet Prince: C

Page 72
Dirty Dishes: A
Puzzled: B

Page 73
A Busy Day: B
Clean Floor: C

Page 74
Costume Party: A
Book Report: B

Page 75
Water Rising: C
Falling like Dominoes: A

Page 76
Where's Mom?: C
Path to Success: B

Page 77
Beautiful Morning: A
Top Five: B

Page 78
Black and White: B
Dressing in Layers: A

Page 79
Frozen Bubbles: C
Visiting Mom: A

Page 80
Metamorphosis: B
Masked Men: C

Making Inferences

Page 81
Be My Valentine: A
A Special Day: B

Page 82
Schedule Change: A
Spoiling the Grandkids: C

Page 83
Tough Run: B
Machu Picchu: C

Page 84
Busy Schedule: A
Heading to Luckyville: C

Page 85
Out of Focus: C
Recess Time: A

Page 86
Office Visit: B
Cool Ears: B

Page 87
Helpful Janet: B
Missing Ingredient: C

Page 88
Book Hunting: C
Quick Quiz: A

Page 89
Return of the Monkeys: B
Tiny Dots: A

Page 90
Painting Dolphins: C
Under the Sea: C

Page 91
New Furniture: B
Hungry Man: A

Page 92
Birthday Lunch: B
Collecting Coins: C

Page 93
Something Shiny: A
Drum Lessons: A

Page 94
Science Camp: C
Cooling Off: A

Page 95
Traveling Back in Time: B
Lovely Languages: B

Predicting Outcomes

Page 96
Save Your Work: B
Free Eggs: C

Page 97
No Misspelled Words: B
Shoe Issues: C

Page 98
Island Bound: A
Please, Do Not Touch: B

Page 99
Piles of Papers: A
Staying Fit: C

Page 100
Ready to Rock: A
Family Photos: B

Page 101
Bad Rash: C
Tongue-Twister: A

Page 102
Swimming Safely: C
Finding Volume: B

Page 103
Remote Ruckus: A
Alice's Animals: A

Page 104
Two Brains Are
Better Than One: C
Long Drive South: B

Page 105
Watching the Clock: B
Not Microwave Safe: A

Page 106
Online Invitation: A
Crazy Hair Day: A

Page 107
A Different Point of View: C
Rapping and Rhyming: C

Page 108
Birthday Wishes: A
Pizza Night: B

Page 109
Shedding Skin: B
Family Movie Night: C

Page 110
Runaway Meatball: A
Fast Bike: C